GCSE English

Spelling, Punctuation & Grammar

This book is for anyone doing GCSE English Literature, History,
Geography or Religious Studies — but it's useful
for other GCSE subjects too.

It'll help you earn the 5% of marks awarded for spelling,
punctuation and grammar in your exams.

It's got everything you need to help boost your grade —
clear explanations, handy tips, practice questions and answers.

And of course, we've done our best to make the whole
experience at least vaguely entertaining for you.

The Study Guide

CONTENTS

Section One — Spelling

Section Two — Punctuation

CONTENTS

Published by CGP

Editors:
Heather Gregson
Anthony Muller
Holly Poynton

With thanks to Glenn Rogers and Nicola Woodfin for the proofreading.

ISBN: 978 1 84762 891 6
Website: www.cgpbooks.co.uk
Printed by Elanders Ltd, Newcastle upon Tyne.
Clipart from CorelDRAW®

Based on the classic CGP style created by Richard Parsons.

Introduction to SPaG

Welcome to the magical, mystical world of 'SPaG'. It's a funny kind of non-word that rhymes with 'hag' and 'bag'. It also sounds like something your Italian mamma might make for dinner. Mmm, dinner...

SPaG stands for Spelling, Punctuation and Grammar

1) SPaG marks are given for correct spelling, punctuation and grammar in certain GCSE subjects.

2) The subjects that award separate SPaG marks are:

• English Literature	• Geography
• History	• Religious Studies

Anyone for SPaGhetti?

3) 5% of the total marks for these GCSE subjects will be given for SPaG.

4) Even if a subject doesn't award marks for SPaG, it's still really important to be able to use spelling, punctuation and grammar correctly.

Read the question Carefully

You won't be tested on SPaG for every question, so you need to read the exam paper carefully. Questions with SPaG marks will be clearly marked, like this:

> **2** Explore how prejudice affects the characters in *Of Mice and Men*. Use evidence to back up your answer.
>
> **[40]**
> **(Total for spelling, punctuation and grammar = 6 marks)**
> **(Total for Question 2 = 46 marks)**

This shows how many SPaG marks are available for this question.

SPaG Marks are Really Important

1) 5% doesn't sound like many marks, but it could be the difference between grades.

2) You'll throw away easy marks if you make silly spelling mistakes or forget how to use punctuation and grammar properly.

3) Even if your SPaG is perfect, if an examiner can't read your handwriting, it could still cost you marks.

Some Pages are Great — especially ones about SPaG...

Now that you know what SPaG marks are, you need to make sure that your spelling, punctuation and grammar skills are completely up to scratch. The rest of this book will help you in your quest...

Plurals

When you have two or more of something, you need to change the noun to a plural form. That's where lots of people mess up. Make sure you learn the right plural spellings now.

Most Words Add '-s' to make the Plural

Usually nouns just add '-s' on the end to make them plural.

human ⇨ humans ⟸ '-s' is added to the noun to make it plural. ⇨ place ⇨ places

Some words need '-es'

1) Add 'es' to nouns ending in <u>these letters</u> — '<u>ch</u>', '<u>sh</u>', '<u>s</u>', '<u>x</u>' and '<u>z</u>'.

2) You <u>can't</u> just add '-s' to these nouns because they'd be <u>difficult to say</u>. You need to add '<u>-es</u>' to help you <u>pronounce</u> the word.

watch + '-s' = watchs ✗ ⇨ watch + '-es' = watches ✓

glass + '-s' = glasss ✗ ⇨ glass + '-es' = glasses ✓

box + '-s' = boxs ✗ ⇨ box + '-es' = boxes ✓

"Open your mouth and say 'boxs'."

There are Two Plural Forms for words that End in '-y'

1) Look at the letter <u>in front</u> of the '<u>y</u>'. If it's a <u>vowel</u> — the letters 'a', 'e', 'i', 'o', 'u' — just <u>add</u> '<u>-s</u>'.

key ⇨ keys ⟸ The letter in front of the 'y' is a vowel, so add '-s' to the end. ⇨ play ⇨ plays

A consonant is any letter which isn't a vowel.

2) If the letter <u>in front</u> of the '<u>y</u>' is a <u>consonant</u> — <u>drop</u> the '<u>y</u>' and add '<u>-ies</u>'.

party ⇨ parties ⟸ The letter before 'y' is a consonant, so drop the 'y' and put '-ies' on the end. ⇨ fly ⇨ flies

3) <u>Names</u> are <u>exceptions</u> to this rule — <u>always</u> add an '<u>s</u>' (unless the name <u>ends</u> with '<u>s</u>').

Both Henrys were good at horse riding.

The letter before 'y' is 'r', which is a consonant, but because it's a name, just add an '-s'.

There were four Jameses who became King.

This name ends with 's' so it follows the '-es' rule above — if a word ends in '-s', add '-es' to the plural.

More than one questionnaire — plural forms...

Phew — loads of stuff to learn here. The secret is to take it slowly. Make sure you understand each rule before you move on to the next one. It might help to write a list of nouns and work out how to make them plural.

Plurals

Words that **End** in 'o' can be **Tricky**

Words that end in '<u>o</u>' <u>usually</u> add '<u>-s</u>' to make their plural, e.g. piano<u>s</u>, disco<u>s</u>.
Some words ending in 'o' are <u>different</u> though — they take '<u>-es</u>' instead.

| potatoes | tomatoes | heroes | echoes | dominoes |

Unfortunately, there's <u>no trick</u> to this rule — you just have to <u>remember</u> the <u>exceptions</u>.

Most words **Ending** in '*f*' and '*fe*' add '*-ves*' to make the **Plural**

For these words you need to <u>change</u> the '<u>f</u>' into a '<u>v</u>', and add '<u>-es</u>'.

| life ⇨ lives | loaf ⇨ loaves | shelf ⇨ shelves | wife ⇨ wives |

But there are <u>awkward ones</u> that <u>keep</u> the '<u>f</u>' and just add '<u>s</u>'.

| chiefs | beliefs | proofs | reefs | chefs |

Other words have **Irregular Plurals**

1) Some words <u>don't</u> follow a <u>pattern</u> for making their plurals. Instead of <u>adding</u> or <u>removing</u> letters you might have to <u>change</u> the spelling of the <u>original word</u>.

2) These words change their <u>vowel sound</u> when they become plural:

| woman ⇨ women | mouse ⇨ mice | tooth ⇨ teeth |

3) Some words that come from <u>other languages</u> also have <u>irregular plurals</u>:

| radius ⇨ radii | criterion ⇨ criteria | oasis ⇨ oases |

Some words **Stay** the **Same** in the **Plural**

Don't write 'fishes' — it's really old-fashioned.

Some words don't change at all — they're the <u>same</u> in both <u>singular</u> and <u>plural</u> forms:

| sheep | deer | bison | moose | buffalo | fish |

Practice Questions

Rewrite these nouns to make them plural.

1) class *es*
2) cit*xies*
3) child *ren*
4) tooth *teeth*
5) church *es*
6) claw*s*
7) volcano *es*
8) life *lives*
9) disco *s*
10) *beliefs*
11) deer
12) lad*xies*

Suffixes and Prefixes

You add suffixes and prefixes to a word to change its meaning. Just don't go getting your fixes in a twist — remember that prefixes go at the beginning of a word, and suffixes go at the end.

Prefixes and *Suffixes* are used to make *New Words*

Prefixes and suffixes are <u>letters</u> that don't make any sense by themselves, but when they're <u>added</u> to <u>other words</u>, they <u>change</u> the word's <u>meaning</u>.

Remember — 'pre' = 'before', so prefixes go at the start of words.

'heat' is the root word. ⟹ heat   reheat ⟸ *'re-' is the prefix*

'Garden' is the root word. ⟹ garden   gardener ⟸ *'-er' is the suffix*

Look out for these *Common Prefix Spelling Errors*

The <u>spelling</u> of the root word <u>never changes</u> when a <u>prefix</u> is added, so don't fall into the trap of <u>adding</u> or <u>taking away</u> letters.

Sometimes you need to add a hyphen between the prefix and the word (see p.25).

dis + similar

There's an 's' missing. → disimilar ✗

dissimilar ✓

dis + appearance

There's an extra 's' in this spelling → dissappearance ✗

disappearance ✓

These are right. The spelling of the root word and the prefix hasn't changed.

Learn these *Rules* for *Spelling Suffixes Correctly*

1) If the <u>root word ends</u> in '<u>e</u>' and the first letter of the suffix is a <u>vowel</u>, you need to <u>drop</u> the '<u>e</u>'.

   love + ing ⟹ loving   care + er ⟹ carer

   The <u>exception</u> to this rule is '<u>-able</u>' — <u>don't drop</u> the '<u>e</u>' when you add the suffix. ⟹ changeable

2) If the first letter of the suffix is a <u>consonant</u>, <u>keep</u> the 'e'.

   love + ly ⟹ lovely   care + less ⟹ careless

   There's more about how spellings change with suffixes on the next page.

3) Make sure you spell the suffix '<u>-ful</u>' with only <u>one</u> '<u>l</u>' — e.g. hopeful, not hopefull.

4) The suffixes '<u>-tion</u>', '<u>-sion</u>' and '<u>-cian</u>' all sound like '<u>-shun</u>'. Make sure you've got the <u>right one</u>.

5) If a <u>root word ends</u> with a consonant and then a '<u>y</u>' you <u>almost always</u> have to <u>change</u> the '<u>y</u>' to an '<u>i</u>' before adding any suffix except '<u>-ing</u>'.   heavy ⟹ heavier

6) If the letter before 'y' is a <u>vowel</u>, you almost always <u>leave</u> the 'y' as it is.   boy ⟹ boyish

Great things don't end in '-ness' — they end in '-fest' or '-mania'...

There are no exceptions to the prefix rule — the root word always stays the same, so make sure you stick to it. Unfortunately for suffixes there's no other alternative than to learn all the oddities and curiosities. Sorry...

Double Letters

Double letters — making spelling double the fun since 1476. These cheeky beggars pop up everywhere, so you need to watch out for them. Missing out a letter is an easy mistake to make, but it could prove costly...

Words with **Double Letters** can be **Tricky**

Try using mnemonics to help you remember these spellings (see p.16).

1) Words with <u>double letters</u> are hard to spell because you say <u>double letters</u> as a <u>single sound</u>.

2) The only thing you can do to <u>remember</u> how to <u>spell</u> these words is to <u>learn them</u>:

accommodation	different	essential	immediately	possess
address	disappear	eventually	necessary	succeed
association	embarrass	exaggerate	occasion	success

Use the **C-V-C Rule** for **Double Letters** and **Suffixes**

1) Use the <u>C-V-C rule</u> to work out whether to <u>double</u> the <u>last letter</u> of a root word when you add a suffix.

The letters 'c', 'h', 'q', 'w', 'x' and 'y' are rarely (or never) doubled when a suffix is added.

2) If the <u>first syllable</u> of a word is <u>stressed</u> (e.g. <u>vi</u>sit or <u>hap</u>pen) you <u>don't</u> double the last letter of the root word when you add a <u>suffix</u>.

⟹ visiting   happening

3) If the <u>last syllable</u> of the root word is <u>stressed</u>, follow this C-V-C rule. If you are adding a suffix which <u>starts with a vowel</u>, look at the <u>last three letters</u> of the <u>root word</u>. If the last three letters go <u>consonant</u> - <u>vowel</u> - <u>consonant</u>, you need to <u>double</u> the last letter.

regret + -ing

'regret' is the root word. Its last syllable is stressed.   '-ing' is the suffix.

r e g r e t   ⟸ 't' is also a consonant.

'r' is a consonant.   'e' is a vowel.

regretting

'regret' fits the C-V-C rule, so the last letter is doubled.

4) If the <u>first letter</u> of the suffix <u>isn't a vowel</u> you <u>don't</u> need to double the last letter.

regret + -ful

'regret' is still the root word.   '-ful' is the suffix.

-ful

'f' is a consonant, so the suffix doesn't begin with a vowel.

regretful

The C-V-C rule does not apply, so the last letter isn't doubled.

Practice Questions

Add the prefixes in brackets to each of the words below. Make sure you check any double letters.

1) *(in) numerable*   3) *(un) necessary*   5) *(un) timely*   7) *(sub) marine*

2) *(dis) approve*   4) *(pro) creation*   6) *(im) maturity*   8) *(ir) relevant*

Using the C-V-C rule, add the suffixes in brackets to the words below. Be sure to check your spelling.

1) *success (ful)*   3) *thought (less)*   5) *budget (ed)*   7) *begin (er)*

2) *forget (ing)*   4) *conquer (ed)*   6) *forgot (en)*   8) *follow (ed)*

Silent Letters and Unstressed Vowels

If you listen carefully you might just hear your name being called on the wind... Not really. And you can't quite make out silent letters and unstressed vowels in words either — they're just as annoying as I am.

Some words have **Silent Letters**

1) Silent letters are <u>letters</u> which you <u>don't hear</u>. Because you can't hear them, it makes words <u>tricky</u> to <u>spell</u>.

2) Make sure you <u>learn</u> the <u>correct spellings</u> of <u>common words</u> with silent letters for your exam — it's an <u>obvious mistake</u> for the examiner to notice.

Learn the **Correct Spelling** of these words

Here are some <u>common examples</u> of words with <u>silent letters</u> — loads more have them, but these are the <u>main ones</u>:

Words with a silent 'h'

which	whether	when
while	chemist	white

Words with a silent 'k'

kneel	knife	knight
knot	know	knowledge

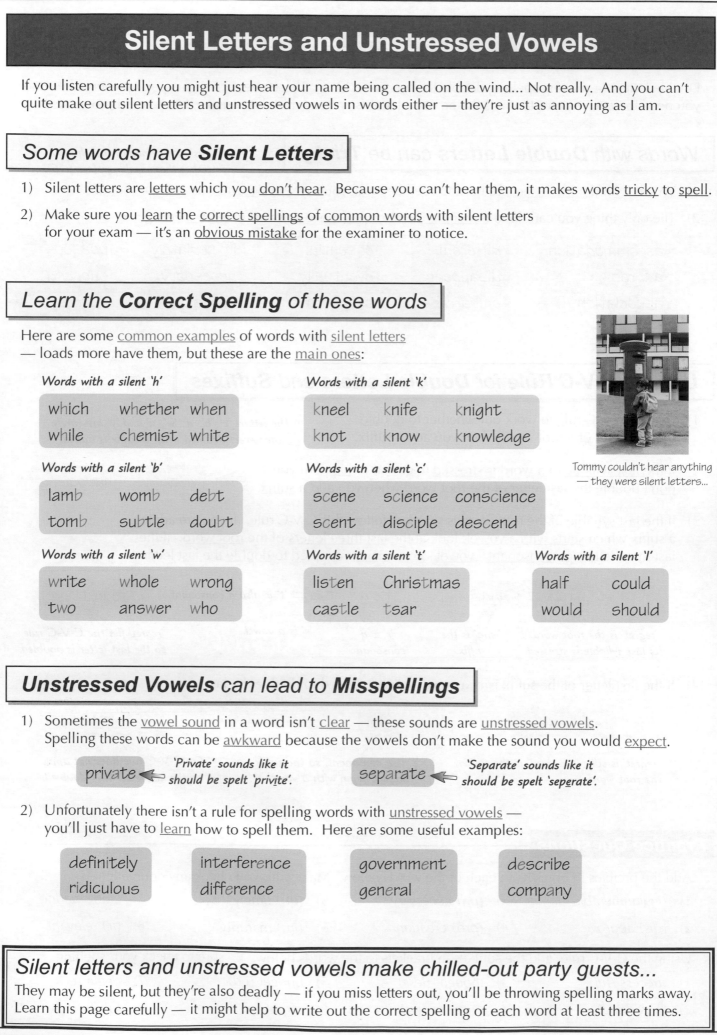

Tommy couldn't hear anything — they were silent letters...

Words with a silent 'b'

lamb	womb	debt
tomb	subtle	doubt

Words with a silent 'c'

scene	science	conscience
scent	disciple	descend

Words with a silent 'w'

write	whole	wrong
two	answer	who

Words with a silent 't'

listen	Christmas
castle	tsar

Words with a silent 'l'

half	could
would	should

Unstressed Vowels can lead to *Misspellings*

1) Sometimes the <u>vowel sound</u> in a word isn't <u>clear</u> — these sounds are <u>unstressed vowels</u>. Spelling these words can be <u>awkward</u> because the vowels don't make the sound you would <u>expect</u>.

private ← *'Private' sounds like it should be spelt 'privite'.*

separate ← *'Separate' sounds like it should be spelt 'seperate'.*

2) Unfortunately there isn't a rule for spelling words with <u>unstressed vowels</u> — you'll just have to <u>learn</u> how to spell them. Here are some useful examples:

definitely	interference	government	describe
ridiculous	difference	general	company

Silent letters and unstressed vowels make chilled-out party guests...

They may be silent, but they're also deadly — if you miss letters out, you'll be throwing spelling marks away. Learn this page carefully — it might help to write out the correct spelling of each word at least three times.

i Before e Rule

This page is about the 'i before e' rule, and its exceptions. It's a confusing rule, but if you don't know it then writing sentences like, "Scientists believe the thief seized eight of his neighbour's glaciers." can be a bit tricky.

The 'i' before 'e' rule

1) 'i' and 'e' often appear together, so it's easy to confuse which way round they are spelt.

2) Use the 'i' before 'e' rule to help you remember how to spell words where 'i' and 'e' appear together.

'i' before 'e' except after 'c', but only when it rhymes with bee. ← The whole word doesn't need to rhyme with bee, just the 'ie' sound.

believe ← The 'ie' sound rhymes with bee, so 'i' goes before 'e'. → thief   receive ← The 'ie' sound rhymes with bee, and there's a 'c', so the 'i' goes after the 'e'.

science ← 'i' comes after 'c', but it doesn't rhyme with bee, so 'i' goes before 'e'.   neighbour ← The 'ie' sound doesn't rhyme with bee, so 'e' goes before 'i'. → eight

Learn the Exceptions to the Rule

Not all words spelt with 'i' and 'e' follow this rule — there are a few exceptions that you need to learn:

glacier ← This exception puts 'i' before 'e' even though it comes after 'c' and rhymes with bee.   weir   weird   seize ← Exceptions that put 'e' before 'i' that rhyme with bee

Words with a Prefix or a Suffix can Break the Rule

1) Adding a prefix or suffix to a word will sometimes break the 'i before e' rule:

queue → queueing   fancy → fancied

suffice → sufficient   insure → reinsure

2) Just remember that prefixes and suffixes have their own spelling rules (see p.4-5), and they take priority over the 'i before e' rule.

Practice Questions

Write out the correct spelling in each of the examples below.

1) goverment / government
2) det / debt
3) believe / beleive
4) assended / ascended
5) species / speceis
6) could / coud
7) wen / when
8) atheists / athiests
9) sutle / subtle
10) deity / diety
11) seperately / separately
12) sceintific / scientific

Forming Comparatives

Comparing one thing to another will be useful in your essays, but forming comparatives incorrectly leads to all sorts of problems. So read this page and learn how to do it properly.

There are **Two Main Ways** to **Compare Things**

1) For <u>short words</u> like 'tall', 'short', 'happy' and 'big', take the <u>adjective</u> and add the <u>suffix</u> '<u>-er</u>' to the <u>end</u>, followed by '<u>than</u>'.

Remember the rules for spelling words with suffixes — see p.4-5.

> Asia is bigger than Europe.

> Jacob is happier than Esau.

An adjective describes a noun.

2) When you're comparing <u>longer words</u> you don't need to add '<u>-er</u>'.

3) If you want to say the <u>first</u> thing is <u>better</u> or <u>bigger</u> than the <u>second</u>:

> Steinbeck is more popular than Salinger. ✓

> Steinbeck is popularer than Salinger. ✗

'more' goes in front of the adjective 'popular'.

'than' goes after the adjective.

Adding '-er' to the adjective gives you a word that doesn't exist.

4) If you want to say the <u>first</u> thing <u>isn't as good</u> or that the <u>two things</u> are the <u>same</u>:

> Steinbeck is less popular than Salinger.

> Steinbeck is as popular as Salinger.

Put 'less' in front of the adjective instead of 'more'.

Put 'as' before and after the adjective.

Learn these **Common Forms** for **Best** and **Worst**

1) Sometimes comparing two things isn't <u>enough</u> — you need to say which is the <u>best</u> or <u>worst</u>. Learn these <u>common forms</u>.

You don't need to do anything to the words in the left-hand box.

'The Crucible' is good.

Adjective	Comparative	Superlative
good	better	best
bad	worse	worst
much / many	more	most
little	less	least
few	fewer	fewest

The words in the right-hand box are superlatives, which are 'most words' — you don't need any other comparative words, but you need to use 'the'.

'The Crucible' is the best.

With the words in the middle box you need to put 'than' after them, otherwise the sentence won't make any sense.

'The Crucible' is better than '1984'.

2) Be careful <u>not to confuse</u> comparatives — you <u>can't</u> say things like 'more better' or 'worst than'.

It was the best of pages, it was the worst...

Watch out for the big mistake — remember that you'll probably need to put in the 'than' and the second thing you're comparing when you use 'more' or 'less'. Without it you might not be writing a proper sentence.

Forming Comparatives

There are **Two Ways** of saying something is the **Most**

1) One way of saying something has the <u>most</u> of a <u>characteristic</u> is to put '<u>-est</u>' on the <u>end</u> of an adjective.

You can only use this method for short adjectives.

2) You should treat '<u>-est</u>' just like any other <u>suffix</u> — it follows the same <u>spelling rules</u> (see p.4-5).

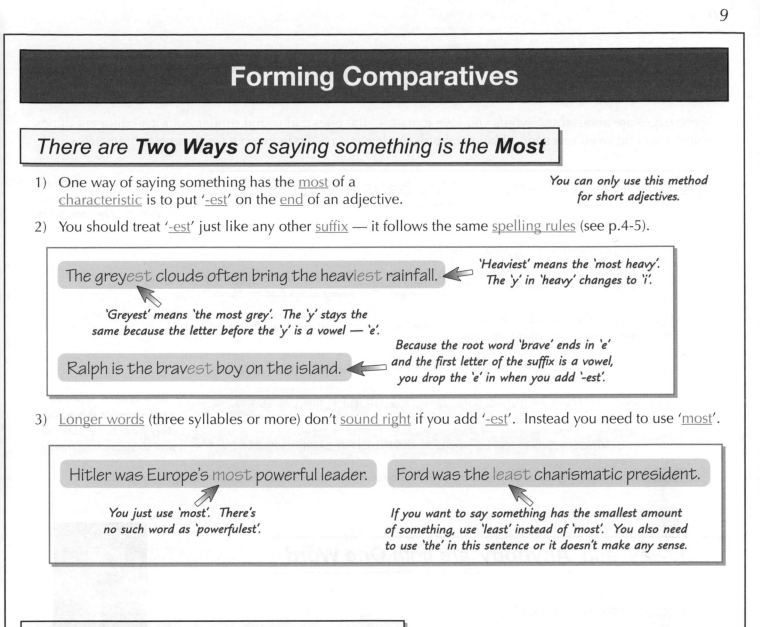

The greyest clouds often bring the heaviest rainfall.

'Heaviest' means the 'most heavy'. The 'y' in 'heavy' changes to 'i'.

'Greyest' means 'the most grey'. The 'y' stays the same because the letter before the 'y' is a vowel — 'e'.

Ralph is the bravest boy on the island.

Because the root word 'brave' ends in 'e' and the first letter of the suffix is a vowel, you drop the 'e' in when you add '-est'.

3) <u>Longer words</u> (three syllables or more) don't <u>sound right</u> if you add '<u>-est</u>'. Instead you need to use '<u>most</u>'.

Hitler was Europe's most powerful leader.

You just use 'most'. There's no such word as 'powerfulest'.

Ford was the least charismatic president.

If you want to say something has the smallest amount of something, use 'least' instead of 'most'. You also need to use 'the' in this sentence or it doesn't make any sense.

Never use '**Most**' and '**-est**' Together

You can either use '<u>most</u>' or add '<u>-est</u>' on the <u>end</u> of your <u>adjective</u> — don't use them <u>both together</u>.

The most earliest version of Romeo and Juliet was printed in 1597. ✗

You don't need 'most' here — 'earliest' already means 'most early'.

Remember that the 'y' in early changes to an 'i' when you add the suffix '-est'.

The earliest version of Romeo and Juliet was printed in 1597. ✓

Practice Questions

Correct each of the sentences below so that the comparatives make sense and are spelt correctly.

1) *'Romeo and Juliet' is <u>most</u> popular than 'Macbeth' in schools, maybe because the story is <u>more good</u>.*

2) *In Geography, the <u>bestest</u> way to get a <u>betterer</u> mark than my friends is to do the <u>more</u> studying.*

3) *China has the <u>most largest</u> population in the world, with <u>most than</u> 1.3 billion people.*

4) *Morale was very important in the trenches — <u>more happier</u> soldiers meant <u>more effecter</u> offensives.*

Commonly Misused Words

These pages are about those words you love to hate — the ones that sound similar but mean different things. Sometimes one word can sound like two words, and vice versa, so watch out for these common errors.

'Maybe' is an Adverb but 'May be' is a Verb Phrase

Adverbs give more information about a verb. E.g. 'He sang quietly' or 'They ran quickly'.

1) 'Maybe' is one word, but 'may be' is two words — they have different meanings.

2) 'Maybe' is an adverb which means 'perhaps'.

> Maybe the young lovers had no choice. ⇐ *This means that perhaps the young lovers had no choice.*

Maybe modifies the verb 'had'. Without it, the sentence means something different. ⇒ The young lovers had no choice.

3) 'May be' is a verb phrase — it means that something is only a possibility.

> Charles I may be the least popular monarch in English History. ⇐ *Both of these sentences means similar things, but they have to be phrased and structured differently.*

> Maybe Charles I is the least popular monarch in English History. ⇐

If you can replace 'may be' with 'might be' and the sentence still makes sense, then you're using the right one.

'Anyway' and 'Anybody' are both One Word

1) 'Anyway' is an adverb which means 'regardless' — it's spelt as one word. 'Any way' means 'any method' — it's spelt as two separate words.

> It was a difficult exam, but I did well anyway. ⇐ *The exam was hard, but I did well regardless.*

This question is asking if there is any method that would allow him to work tomorrow. ⇒ Is there any way he can work tomorrow?

I don't have any body.

2) 'Everybody' is a pronoun which means 'every person' — it's spelt as one word. 'Every body' means 'every group' or 'every physical body' — it's spelt as two separate words.

> Do you know where everybody is? ⇐ *This question is asking where all the people are.*

> Every body of power has to make rules.   Every body needs minerals and vitamins.

In this context 'every body' means 'any group'.   *In this context 'every body' means 'every physical body'.*

3) The same idea applies to 'anybody' and 'any body'. 'Anybody' means 'any person', 'any body' means 'any group' or 'any physical body'.

This page may be the funniest in the whole book. Or maybe not...

It makes you wonder why they couldn't make up new words for all these things instead of sticking two old words together — it would have saved a lot of trouble. You'll get the hang of them if you keep plugging away.

Commonly Misused Words

'Always' and *'Altogether'* are **Adverbs**

1) 'Always' and 'altogether' are both spelt as <u>one word</u> — don't confuse them with 'all ways' and 'all together'.

2) 'Always' means 'at all times', but 'all ways' means 'every way' or the 'total number of methods'.

> Atticus always fights for justice.

Atticus fights for justice at every opportunity.

> All ways out of the city are blocked.

Every way (or route) is blocked.

3) 'Altogether' means 'completely' or 'in total'. 'All together' means 'at the same time', 'in the same place' or 'in a group'.

> I have nine albums altogether.

This is the number of albums in total.

> I am altogether exhausted.

This means 'completely exhausted'.

> Let's jump all together.

This means 'let's jump all at the same time'.

'Into' is a **Preposition** or **Part** of a **Verb**

A preposition is a word which tells you where, when or how something happened.

1) 'Into' is a <u>preposition</u> which shows that something is <u>moving towards</u> the <u>inside</u> of <u>something</u>.

> The boy ran into the house.

These examples show the direction of the boy and the plug.

> The plug went into the socket.

If you can <u>replace</u> 'into' with the word 'inside' and it still makes <u>sense</u>, you're using it <u>correctly</u>.

2) 'Into' is also part of the verb 'to turn into'.

> He turned into a monster.

3) 'In' and 'to' are spelt as two separate words when the 'to' belongs to a <u>verb</u>.

> They came in to look around.

'to' belongs to the verb 'look'. It's part of an infinitive verb.

An infinitive verb is the most basic form of a verb with the word 'to' in front of it, e.g. 'to see'.

If you replace 'in' with 'inside', you still need the word 'to'.

4) 'In' and 'to' can be spelt as two separate words when the 'to' is a <u>preposition</u>.

> She turned her homework in to her teacher.

This sentence means she gave her homework to her teacher.

If you use 'into' by mistake, the sentence means something completely different — the homework was transformed into her teacher.

> She turned her homework into her teacher.

Practice Questions

Rewrite these sentences using the correct underlined word or words so that they make most sense.

1) *I <u>may be</u>/<u>maybe</u> able to help, but then again <u>may be</u>/<u>maybe</u> not.*

2) *Is there <u>anyway</u>/<u>any way</u> to drill <u>in to</u>/<u>into</u> the depths of the deepest glaciers?*

3) *I was <u>all together</u>/<u>altogether</u> confused by her attempt to turn a rabbit <u>into</u>/<u>in to</u> a dove.*

4) *They came <u>into</u>/<u>in to</u> investigate <u>every body's</u>/<u>everybody's</u> alibis.*

Section One — Spelling

Commonly Misused Words

These words won't be happy chappies if you misuse them. So be careful in your writing, and make sure to learn the differences between them and practise using them. It's as simple as that.

Practise is a *Verb* but *Practice* is a *Noun*

<u>Practise</u> is a <u>doing word</u>, which means it's a <u>verb</u> — it's spelt with an '<u>s</u>'.

The boys practise hunting.	She is practising the piano.

<u>Practice</u> is <u>something</u> you <u>go to</u>, so it's a <u>noun</u> — it's spelt with a '<u>c</u>'.

The boys have hunting practice.	Tennis practice is hard work.

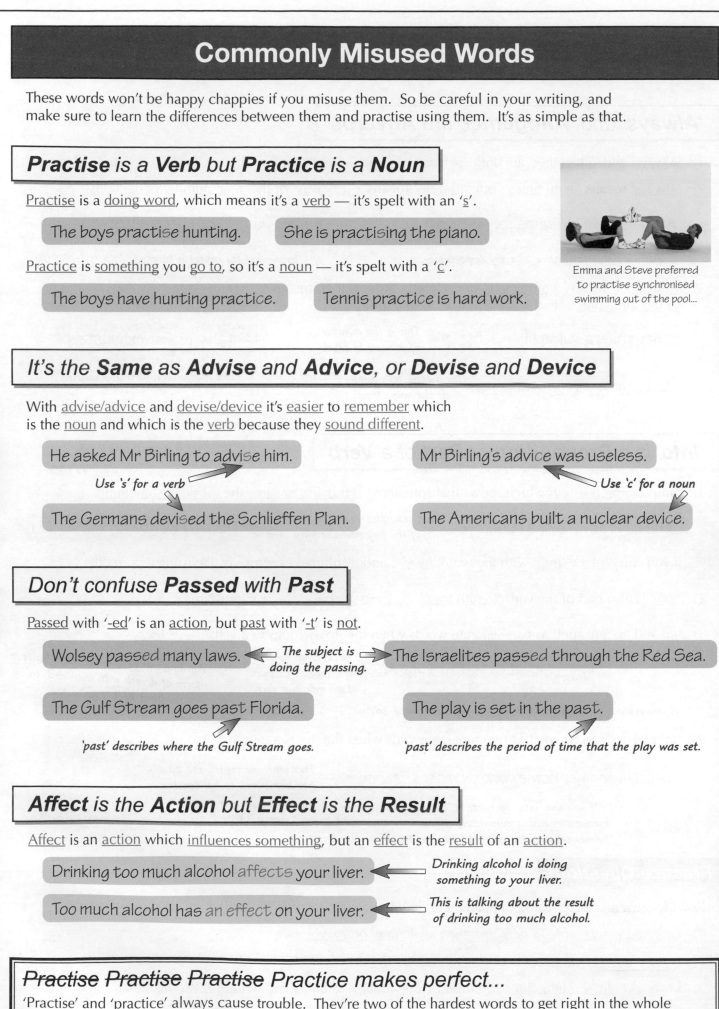

Emma and Steve preferred to practise synchronised swimming out of the pool...

It's the **Same** *as* **Advise** *and* **Advice**, *or* **Devise** *and* **Device**

With <u>advise/advice</u> and <u>devise/device</u> it's <u>easier</u> to <u>remember</u> which is the <u>noun</u> and which is the <u>verb</u> because they <u>sound different</u>.

He asked Mr Birling to advise him.

Use 's' for a verb

The Germans devised the Schlieffen Plan.

Mr Birling's advice was useless.

Use 'c' for a noun

The Americans built a nuclear device.

Don't confuse **Passed** *with* **Past**

<u>Passed</u> with '<u>-ed</u>' is an <u>action</u>, but <u>past</u> with '<u>-t</u>' is <u>not</u>.

Wolsey passed many laws. *The subject is doing the passing.* The Israelites passed through the Red Sea.

The Gulf Stream goes past Florida.

'past' describes where the Gulf Stream goes.

The play is set in the past.

'past' describes the period of time that the play was set.

Affect is the *Action* but *Effect* is the *Result*

<u>Affect</u> is an <u>action</u> which <u>influences something</u>, but an <u>effect</u> is the <u>result</u> of an <u>action</u>.

Drinking too much alcohol affects your liver.

Drinking alcohol is doing something to your liver.

Too much alcohol has an effect on your liver.

This is talking about the result of drinking too much alcohol.

~~Practise Practise Practise~~ Practice makes perfect...

'Practise' and 'practice' always cause trouble. They're two of the hardest words to get right in the whole English language. Remember, 'practice' is a thing, an event or an idea. 'Practise' is a verb. Basil is a herb.

Commonly Misused Words

Accept *is* Totally Different *to* Except

1) <u>Accept</u> is a <u>verb</u> — it means to '<u>agree</u>' with something or to '<u>receive</u>' something.

> Most scholars accept that a man named Jesus existed. ← *This means that scholars agree that a man called Jesus existed.*

2) <u>Except</u> means '<u>not including</u>'.

> *This means that only Ralph didn't turn to savagery.* → Everyone turns to savagery except Ralph.

Where, Were *and* Wear

These three words <u>sound similar</u>, but they have very <u>different meanings</u>.

1) <u>Where</u> is used for <u>places</u> and <u>positions</u>.   Where is Mumbai?

2) <u>Wear</u> is what you do with <u>clothes</u>, <u>shoes</u> and <u>jewellery</u>.   I wear my costume.

3) <u>Were</u> is the <u>past form</u> of <u>are</u>.   They were studying glaciers. ← *If you're not sure about 'were' in a sentence, use 'are' instead. If it still makes sense then 'were' is probably right.*

There, Their *and* They're

Make sure you use these <u>three correctly</u> — it's really <u>obvious</u> to the examiner if you <u>confuse</u> them.

1) <u>There</u> goes with <u>where</u> — it's about <u>places</u> and <u>positions</u>.   There is evidence to support this.

2) <u>Their</u> means it <u>belongs</u> to <u>them</u>.   Their sacred text is the Qur'an.

3) <u>They're</u> is <u>short</u> for '<u>they are</u>'.   They're still researching climate change.

'They're' is too informal for exams — use 'they are' instead.

Practice Questions

Rewrite these sentences using the correctly spelt underlined word.

1) <u>They're</u>/<u>Their</u> aim was to avoid the impact of war, but it still had an <u>affect</u>/<u>effect</u> on the country.

2) In the <u>passed</u>/<u>past</u>, Jews <u>where</u>/<u>were</u> discouraged from marrying someone from another religious faith.

3) The Inspector is a plot <u>device</u>/<u>devise</u> designed to force the Birlings to <u>accept</u>/<u>except</u> their wrongdoings.

4) It is important to <u>practice</u>/<u>practise</u> emergency drills in countries <u>wear</u>/<u>where</u> earthquakes are common.

Commonly Misused Words

More of the same on these pages, I'm afraid. It turns out a lot of words in the English language get mixed up, but I'm confident that after these pages I'll never misuse a word again, so lettuce begin...

To / Too / Two — they're All Different

This one's a really common mistake, so make sure you don't slip up:

1) To means 'towards' or is part of a verb.

   They're going to Geneva. ← 'to' means 'in the direction of'.

   He wants to reform. ← 'to' is part of the verb 'to reform'.

2) Two is just the number '2'. Two million pounds ← It might help to think of 'tw' for 'twice'.

3) Too means 'too much' or 'also'.

   This novel's too long... ← This means that the novel is overly long.

   ... and it's boring too. ← This means that it is also boring.

Off means 'Away From' or 'Not On' — the rest of the time use Of

Off means 'away from' or 'not on'. Of is just a linking word:

This means 35% taken away from the price. → All items 35% off

The lights were off. ← This means the lights were 'not on'.

Snowball is full of ideas. ← 'of' links the words together. → A man of morals

Our is a Pronoun and Are is a Verb

'Our' is a possessive pronoun (see p.32). 'Are' is a present tense form of the verb 'to be' (see p.37).

It is our decision. ← 'our' means that the decision belongs to them.

We are deciding. ← 'are' tells you what the subject of the sentence is doing.

'A lot' is Always written as Two Words

A common mistake to make is writing 'alot' instead of 'a lot' — 'alot' is never correct.

There are alot of reasons. ✗ ← Never write this as one word.

There are a lot of reasons. ✓

Two sets of identical twins make it too difficult to remember who's who...

There's a lot to get your head round here but it's worth learning — even if it is very confusing. You'd think that the English language would have enough letters to avoid repeating itself. I blame society.

Commonly Misused Words

Watch out for **Though**, **Thought**, **Through** and **Thorough**

These words all look similar, so it's easy to write the wrong one by mistake, but it could cost you if you do.

Electric cars are a good idea, though they have their drawbacks. ⇐ 'Though' means 'however'.

I thought about the exam. ⇐ 'Thought' is the past tense of the verb 'to think'.

I had a thought. ⇐ Or 'a thought' can be 'an idea'.

'Through' means 'going from one side of something to the other'. ⇒ It went through the window.

He was thorough in his work. ⇐ 'Thorough' means 'careful' or 'in depth'.

Don't use '**Them**' when you **Mean** '**Those**'

For more on pronouns see p.32-33.

1) 'Them' is a pronoun — never use it with the noun it replaces.

2) 'Those' is used to point out specific things.

I hate them scenes. ✗ ⇐ In this example, 'them' has been used when it should be 'those'. You can't use 'them' and 'scenes' together.

I hate those scenes. ✓ ↖ This is right.

I hate them. ✓ ⇐ This is also OK, as long as the reader knows what 'them' refers to.

Teach and **Learn** are **Opposites**

Teaching means 'giving out knowledge', and learning means 'to take in knowledge'.

Can you learn me to spell? ✗

This doesn't make sense as you want them to do the teaching, not the learning.

Can you teach me to spell? ✓

This does make sense — you're doing the learning, they're doing the teaching.

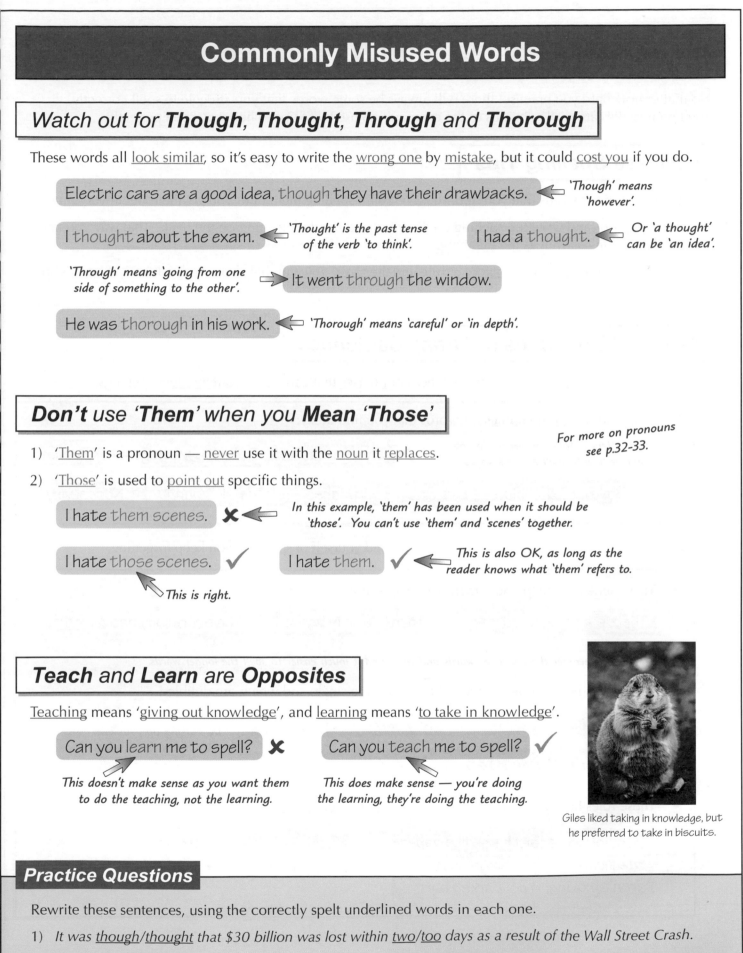

Giles liked taking in knowledge, but he preferred to take in biscuits.

Practice Questions

Rewrite these sentences, using the correctly spelt underlined words in each one.

1) It was though/thought that $30 billion was lost within two/too days as a result of the Wall Street Crash.

2) The values in 'To Kill a Mockingbird' will learn/teach you a lot because many of them/those are still relevant.

3) Our/Are research into renewable energy has been very through/thorough in the last few years.

4) The teachings off/of Judaism and Islam are against euthanasia. Catholics are opposed two/to it too/to.

Section One — Spelling

Spelling Tricky Words

No matter how hard you practise, there will always be some words that you struggle to spell correctly. Spelling mistakes are really obvious to the examiner, so use these tips to help you spell perfectly.

Use these **Spelling Tips**

1) Keep a <u>list</u> of the words that you find <u>tricky</u>. <u>Practise</u> spelling them until you get them right <u>every time</u>.

2) Use <u>flashcards</u> and write the spelling on the front, and put the <u>meaning</u> on the <u>back</u>. That way you can <u>test</u> the <u>spelling</u> as well as the <u>meaning</u>.

3) <u>Learn spelling rules</u> — the '<u>i before e</u>' rule and the <u>C-V-C rule</u> can help you work out how a word is spelt.

Make up **Mnemonics** or **Funny Sentences**

1) Try using <u>mnemonics</u> — these are <u>sentences</u> or <u>phrases</u> that can <u>help</u> you <u>remember</u> spellings.

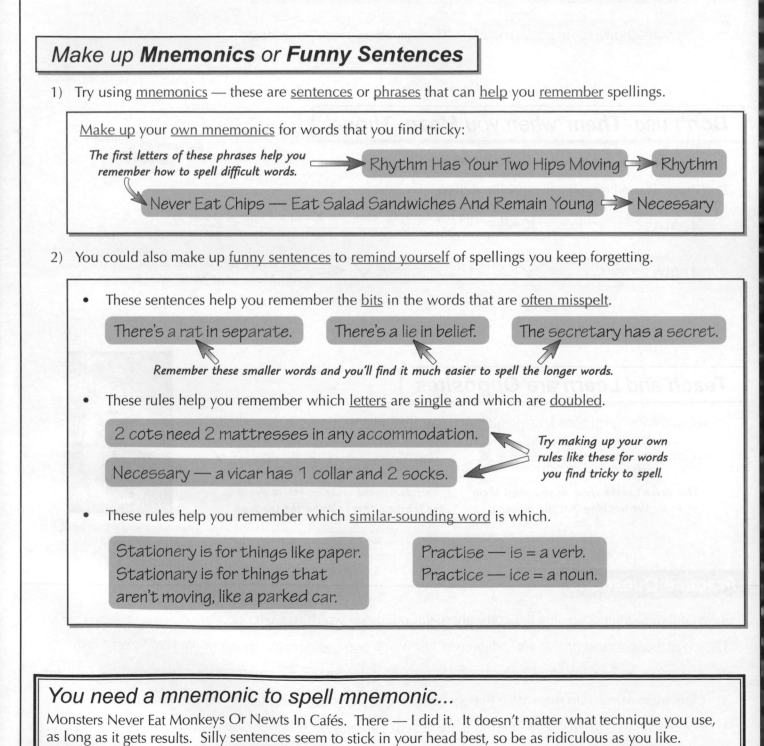

<u>Make up</u> your <u>own mnemonics</u> for words that you find tricky:

The first letters of these phrases help you remember how to spell difficult words.

Rhythm Has Your Two Hips Moving ⟹ Rhythm

Never Eat Chips — Eat Salad Sandwiches And Remain Young ⟹ Necessary

2) You could also make up <u>funny sentences</u> to <u>remind yourself</u> of spellings you keep forgetting.

- These sentences help you remember the <u>bits</u> in the words that are <u>often misspelt</u>.

There's a rat in separate.   There's a lie in belief.   The secretary has a secret.

Remember these smaller words and you'll find it much easier to spell the longer words.

- These rules help you remember which <u>letters</u> are <u>single</u> and which are <u>doubled</u>.

2 cots need 2 mattresses in any accommodation.

Necessary — a vicar has 1 collar and 2 socks.

Try making up your own rules like these for words you find tricky to spell.

- These rules help you remember which <u>similar-sounding word</u> is which.

Stationery is for things like paper. Stationary is for things that aren't moving, like a parked car.

Practise — is = a verb.
Practice — ice = a noun.

You need a mnemonic to spell mnemonic...

Monsters Never Eat Monkeys Or Newts In Cafés. There — I did it. It doesn't matter what technique you use, as long as it gets results. Silly sentences seem to stick in your head best, so be as ridiculous as you like.

Spelling Tricky Words

Spell Sensibly in the Exam

Even if you've <u>prepared properly</u>, there's still a chance that your mind might go <u>blank</u> in the exam.
The important thing is <u>not to panic</u> — remember this <u>simple advice</u> to help you get those SPaG marks:

1) If you're <u>quoting</u> from <u>source material</u> in the exam, <u>check</u> your spelling against the extract.
   The examiner won't be impressed if you <u>misspell</u> a word that you've been <u>given</u>.

2) If you're <u>struggling</u> to spell a word — <u>sound it out</u> in your head. Work
   out how <u>each syllable</u> sounds and have a <u>sensible go</u> at spelling it.

3) <u>Write out</u> any troublesome words in <u>rough</u>, to see whether
   they <u>look right</u> before you use them in your essay.

4) If you're still <u>not sure</u> how to spell a word, try to use a <u>different word</u>
   that <u>means the same</u>, and that you definitely <u>know</u> how to spell.

5) Even if you're <u>not sure</u> whether you've spelt a word correctly, <u>stick</u> to
   the spelling you've chosen. It's obvious to the examiner that you've
   made a mistake if you spell the <u>same word</u> in three <u>different ways</u>.

"Brian, you idiot, it was supposed
to say 'We love coleslaw...'"

6) If you notice a <u>mistake</u>, put a <u>neat line</u> through the word and <u>rewrite</u> it clearly above.

*See p.52-53 for more
on correcting mistakes.*

Learn these Common Exam Words

*If you're not sure which words you struggle with,
have a look through some old homework to see
which mistakes your teacher keeps correcting.*

Some words come up in <u>essays</u> time and time again, so make sure you get them <u>learnt</u>.

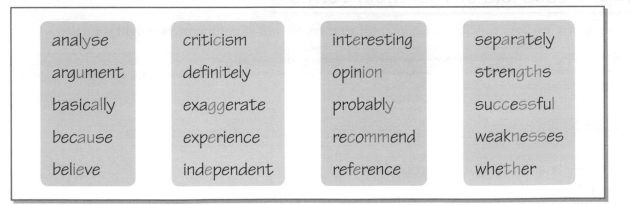

analyse	criticism	interesting	separately
argument	definitely	opinion	strengths
basically	exaggerate	probably	successful
because	experience	recommend	weaknesses
believe	independent	reference	whether

Practice Questions

Write down a mnemonic or silly rule to help you remember how to spell each of these difficult words.

1) *strengths*

2) *exaggerate*

3) *basically*

4) *analyse*

5) *probably*

6) *recommend*

7) *reference*

8) *definitely*

9) *separately*

10) *successful*

11) *criticism*

12) *interesting*

Misspelt History and Geography Words

These pages contain some tricky words that you might need in your exam. They're just a starting point though — make sure you make your own vocab lists for the subjects you're taking, so you can impress the examiner.

History uses fairly **Uncommon** words

Only learn the words that you'll need for the subjects you're taking.

You might have heard some of these words in everyday usage, but some of them seem to be stuck between the pages of History textbooks. You need to know what they mean, as well as how to spell them:

- artillery — large guns used in warfare, particularly for bombardment
- biased — when a source has been affected by the author's opinion
- democracy — a system of government where people elect representatives to political office
- government — the people who hold political office and who govern a country
- hyperinflation — when money inflates at a very fast rate, and loses a lot of its value
- parliament — an institution where the elected government meets to debate and pass laws
- propaganda — information that is usually biased, used to promote a particular group
- reliability — how reliable a source might be
- suffrage — the right to vote in elections (suffragettes are people who promote this right)

Geography uses lots of **Technical Terms**

Some of these words are very specific to Geography, so if you've not learnt them you might struggle:

- businesses — more than one commercial company or business
- desert — a large, dry, barren area of land
- development — the improvement, advancement or progression of something
- environment — the natural world around us
- hydraulic — when liquid moves in a confined space, under intense pressure
- trade bloc — when a group of countries reduce trade barriers between them
- vegetation — the collection of plants found in a particular area
- volcano — a rupture in the Earth's crust that allows lava and hot gas to escape

There are just not enough graphs in Geography — or stories in History...

There are loads more hard-to-spell words in these subjects that aren't here — you've still got to learn them or you may lose marks. The only surefire way to be covered is to learn the dictionary, but I don't recommend it.

Misspelt English and RS Words

You'll need these words in **English Essays**

Most of these words are <u>technical terms</u> that you'll need to talk about <u>types</u> of <u>writing</u>:

alliteration — when consonants are repeated at the beginnings of nearby words

assonance — when words share the same vowel sound, but the consonants are different

figurative — something that isn't meant to be taken literally

genre — the type of literature a piece is, e.g. romantic, gothic

metaphor — a way of describing something by saying that it is something else

onomatopoeia — when a word sounds like what it means, e.g. fizz, buzz and crash

personification — when you talk about something non-human as if it's a person

rhetorical — a rhetorical question is one which doesn't need an answer

simile — a way of describing something by saying that it is like something else

Religious Studies has a lot of **Long Words**

<u>RS</u> has some of the <u>trickiest</u> words of the bunch — make sure you've got them <u>covered</u>.

atheism — a complete denial of the existence of a god

agnosticism — a belief that it's impossible to know whether or not there's a god

conscience — an inner feeling of what's right and wrong

euthanasia — ending someone's life to relieve their suffering, especially from a terminal illness

omnipotence — having unlimited power so that all things are possible

pacifism — the idea that war and physical violence are wrong under all circumstances

resurrection — being brought back to life after death (either by body or by soul)

Practice Questions

Check each word for spelling mistakes. If any words are spelt incorrectly, rewrite them with the correct spelling.

1) mispelt	5) cieling	9) insightful
2) shelfs	6) alphabetical	10) brushs
3) supposed	7) acept	11) criticism
4) progressing	8) sieze	12) allthough

Capital Letters

Using capital letters seems obvious, but there's more to them than you think. Don't throw away valuable marks by skipping this page because you think you know it — I promise it's useful.

Use **Capitals** at the **Start** of **Sentences**

Make sure that your capital letters are obvious — they should be twice as big as normal letters.

Every sentence <u>starts</u> with a <u>capital letter</u>.

The novel is about racism. It was set in the 1930s, but I think it's still relevant. ✓

Both of these sentences need capital letters at the beginning.　　*'I' has a capital letter wherever you use it.*

Some words **Always** start with a **Capital Letter**

Some words start with a capital letter, even in the <u>middle of a sentence</u>:

1) <u>People's names</u> and <u>titles</u>　　Tsar Nicolas II was unpopular.　　John Proctor faced a choice.

2) Names of <u>organisations</u>　　Royal Geographical Society　　Church of England

3) Titles of <u>books</u> and <u>plays</u>　　Animal Farm　　Lord of the Flies

Short words like 'of', 'the' and 'upon' don't have capital letters.

4) <u>Towns</u> and names of <u>places</u>　　Sheffield　　Kingston upon Thames, London

5) <u>Countries</u> and <u>nationalities</u>　　I am French. I come from France and I speak French.

6) <u>Religions</u>, the <u>names of gods</u> and <u>religious believers</u>　　Islam is a religion and Muslims worship Allah.

7) Names of <u>days</u> and <u>months</u>　　Wednesday　　January　　February

Names for particular people, places and things are called 'proper nouns'.

8) <u>Public holidays</u> and <u>religious days</u>　　Christmas　　Diwali　　Easter

Capitalising some words can be *Tricky*

Some nouns are capitalised <u>sometimes</u>, but <u>not</u> at other times.

Some kings wear crowns.　　　　The King wore his crown.

If you're talking about kings in general, you don't need a capital letter.　　*If you're talking about a particular king, you need a capital letter.*

London is a capital city with a capital 'L'...

Yes, yes, this all seems very simple and easy but you still need to make sure you know when to add a capital letter to the beginning of words. If you don't use them properly, you'll look like a foolish fool indeed.

Ending Sentences

Your motto should be something like, "I've started, so I'll finish (these sentences properly)."
Use punctuation to finish sentences correctly — you'll be throwing marks away if you don't.

Full Stops End sentences

1) Full stops are used to <u>end statements</u>.

2) If you're writing an <u>essay</u>, you'll finish <u>most</u> of your sentences with a full stop.

> The children portray Boo Radley as a monster. This reflects the adults' prejudices. ✓

This is correct — each sentence finishes with a full stop.

Question Marks show the end of a *Question*

1) Question marks show that you're <u>asking a question</u>:

> Why were the 1930s a time of famine?

2) Some sentences tell you <u>about</u> a question but <u>don't</u> actually <u>ask one</u>.

The girls didn't question their outfits until it was too late.

> Ralph asks Jack why he hates him.

This isn't actually asking a question, so there's no question mark. It's a statement about what Ralph does — it just needs a full stop.

Exclamation Marks show *Strong Emotions*

1) <u>Exclamation marks</u> are used to show <u>strong emotions</u>, or to <u>emphasise</u> something.

2) You <u>shouldn't</u> need to use exclamation marks in your essays, unless you're <u>quoting</u> a line which uses one.

> The sheep continue to chant, "Four legs good, two legs better!"

3) If you use exclamation marks in your writing, <u>never</u> use <u>more than one</u> to end a sentence.

> What a surprise!!! ✗   What a surprise! ✓

Don't use exclamation marks too often — they'll lose their impact.

Practice Questions

Rewrite these sentences, adding capital letters, full stops and question marks where they are needed.

1) *in 1941, president roosevelt gave an important speech*

2) *it can be very cold in norway during december*

3) *which characters sometimes speak in latin*

4) *the boys asked whether they could play outside the school*

Commas

Commas, eh... what are they good for? Well, without commas, lists would be a jumbled up mess of words, and your long sentences wouldn't make much sense at all. So, respect the comma and learn how to use it.

Commas Separate items in a List

1) A list that doesn't contain commas is really <u>hard to understand</u>:

> Floods damage houses farms roads and bridges. ✗

2) Add a comma after <u>each item</u> to make your list clear.

3) Put '<u>and</u>' or '<u>or</u>' between the last two items in the list. Remember, you <u>don't</u> need to use a comma before the final '<u>and</u>' or '<u>or</u>'.

> Floods damage houses, farms, roads and bridges. ✓

Jean-Pierre, Richard, Harry and Brian had commas in all the right places.

You only need to use commas in lists of three or more items.

4) Use commas to <u>separate</u> two <u>adjectives</u> next to each other which could be separated by '<u>and</u>'.

> He was a cruel, ruthless king.

You could put 'and' here, so you need a comma.

> It was a light green jumper.

You couldn't put 'and' here, so you don't need a comma.

A Comma combines Two Points

1) Two sentences can be joined using a <u>connective</u>, and sometimes with a <u>comma</u> as well.

2) The most common <u>short connectives</u> are:

> - and
> - but
> - while
> - yet
> - so
> - or

Connectives are linking words that join sentences or parts of sentences together.

3) When these words are used to <u>connect two sentences</u> the comma shows where the <u>next point begins</u>:

> The Sun is lower in the sky, so its heat is spread over more of the Earth's surface.

The comma and 'so' join the two sentences.

> The American economy was stronger by 1935, but some problems remained.

4) <u>Longer linking words</u>, like 'however', 'therefore' and 'nevertheless', are also followed by a comma when they're at the <u>start</u> of a sentence:

> However, Giles Corey is one of the most likeable characters in the play.

NEWSFLASH: Sentences Are Divided Over Shock Comma Break-Up...

Commas are a pesky bunch, but you'll be fine if you use your *comma-n sense* (oh dear). But don't put them in whenever you feel like it — it'll distract your reader from the intelligent, insightful points you're making.

Section Two — Punctuation

Commas

Commas separate Extra Information

1) Use a <u>pair of commas</u> to separate extra information in the <u>middle</u> of a sentence:

> The animals, led by Snowball, planned a revolution.

These commas enclose the extra information — 'led by Snowball'.

2) You can check you've used commas <u>correctly</u> if you can <u>remove</u> the information <u>inside</u> the pair of commas and the sentence still <u>makes sense</u>:

> 'The Crucible', which was written in 1952, was inspired by real events.
>
> *This bit is the extra information — if you remove it, the sentence should still make sense.*
>
> 'The Crucible' was inspired by real events. ✓
>
> *This makes sense, so the commas were used correctly.*

The Extra Information can Begin or End the sentence

1) If the extra information is at the <u>beginning</u> or <u>end</u> of a sentence, you still need to use a <u>comma</u>.

2) In this case you only need to use a <u>single comma</u>, rather than a pair.

> When they had discussed the issues, the leaders signed the agreement.
>
> *This is the extra information, so it's followed by a comma.*
>
> One leader refused to sign the agreement, which caused a problem.
>
> *This time the extra part is at the end of the sentence, so it follows a comma.*

3) You can check that you've put the comma in the right place by removing the extra part:

> One leader refused to sign the agreement. ✓

Practice Questions

Rewrite these sentences, adding a missing comma.

1) *The prophets, Moses and Elijah appeared out of nowhere.*

2) *Germany, France Spain and Italy are European countries.*

3) *Unlike most authors at the time Jane Austen wrote about women.*

4) *The French Prime Minister the British Prime Minister and the President were in agreement.*

5) *The children who had studied the novel, failed to understand it.*

6) *The USA and USSR, despite their history became allies.*

Colons and Semicolons

Semicolons are like strong commas: they make bigger pauses and break up longer lists. Don't use colons or semicolons unless you know what you're doing — it will end in tiny punctuation tears if you get them wrong.

Colons introduce *Information* or *Explanations*

1) You can use a <u>colon</u> to show that what <u>follows</u> gives you <u>more information</u> about the first part of the sentence. This can sometimes take the form of a <u>list</u>:

These are the main themes of the novel: loneliness, prejudice, dreams and death.

The colon goes here, just before the information about the themes.

2) You can also use a colon to <u>introduce an explanation</u> in a sentence:

The bit after the colon doesn't need to be a full sentence by itself.

Tropical rainforests are facing a serious problem: deforestation on a large scale.

This colon introduces an explanation of what the problem is.

Semicolons Join Sentences and *Break Up Lists*

Semicolons will impress the examiner, but only if you use them correctly.

1) Semicolons <u>join two sentences</u> into one <u>longer sentence</u>. The sentences must be about the <u>same thing</u>, and they must both be of <u>equal importance</u>.

Orwell wrote 'Animal Farm' in 1943-44; it was difficult for him to find a publisher.

The semicolon joins these two equally important sentences together.

2) Semicolons also <u>break up</u> lists of <u>long phrases</u>.

In your introduction, outline the main argument of your essay; use separate paragraphs to explain each point clearly; in your conclusion, bring your argument together; if you have time, read your essay to check for mistakes.

You need a semicolon before the 'if'.

Colons and *Semicolons* are used *Differently*

Putting a <u>colon</u> or <u>semicolon</u> into a sentence can <u>change</u> its <u>meaning</u>. A colon <u>introduces an explanation</u> of what comes before it, but a semicolon <u>doesn't</u>.

George was happy; Lennie was thinking about the farm.

The semicolon shows that the two parts are related, but doesn't explain why George is happy.

George was happy: Lennie was thinking about the farm.

The colon shows that Lennie 'thinking about the farm' is the reason for George's happiness.

Use colons properly — don't end your essay with a :-)

Yes, my friend, colons and semicolons aren't just for making winking faces in text messages — they can bag you extra SPaG marks too. A word to the wise: don't use them unless you know you're using them correctly.

Brackets and Hyphens

Brackets are nifty bits of punctuation if you can use them correctly. Just like all great couples (Romeo and Juliet, Elizabeth and Darcy, Barbie and Ken), you should never see one bracket without the other.

Brackets enclose **Extra Information** *in a sentence*

1) Brackets go around extra information to keep it separate.

World War I (1914-1918) had many causes.

This is extra information, so the brackets go around this bit.

Brackets are always used in pairs.

FOR SALE — 2 bedroom house with outside space (roof garden).

2) They can also separate an explanation or definition.

In Christian teachings, marriage is for procreation (to have children).

If the information in brackets is at the end of the sentence, the full stop goes outside the second bracket.

3) Brackets can be used to separate information in a similar way to a pair of commas (see p.23):

If you're not sure whether to use brackets or commas, think about what sounds the most natural:

Brackets work better here... 'Surrender' (a verb) means 'to give up'.

'Surrender', which is a verb, means 'to give up'. *... and commas are better here.*

Hyphens usually **Join** *words together*

1) Hyphens can be used to join a prefix to a root word. This usually happens when the prefix ends with the same letter that the root word starts with.

re-enter   semi-interested   ultra-adventurous

2) Use a hyphen if the word could be mixed up with another word that means something different.

I re-covered the chair. → *This means 'I covered the chair again'.*   I recovered the chair. → *This means 'I got the chair back'.*

3) If the root word starts with a capital letter, use a hyphen to attach the prefix.

pro-Russian   anti-Europe   post-Victorian

Practice Questions

Rewrite these sentences and add a pair of brackets to each sentence.

1) *Elizabeth I was the daughter of Henry VIII and Anne Boleyn (his second wife.)*

2) *Boxer (a cart-horse) is a determined and loyal worker on the farm.*

3) *CAFOD (Catholic Agency for Overseas Development) is a religious charity.*

4) *There is a consensus (general agreement) that glacial retreat is caused by global warming.*

Apostrophes and Missing Letters

When you use a shortened form, like 'we've' instead of 'we have', you need to use an apostrophe to show that there are letters missing. If you don't, the word won't make sense, and nobody wants that.

Apostrophes replace Missing Letters

Shortened words or phrases like 'you've' or 'doesn't' use apostrophes to show where letters have been removed.

Avoid using shortened forms of words like 'we're' and 'they'd' in your essays — it's better to write 'we are' or 'they had'.

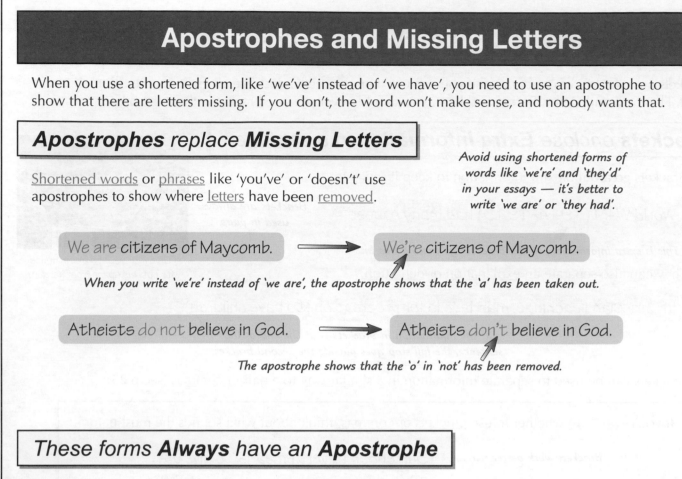

We are citizens of Maycomb. → We're citizens of Maycomb.

When you write 'we're' instead of 'we are', the apostrophe shows that the 'a' has been taken out.

Atheists do not believe in God. → Atheists don't believe in God.

The apostrophe shows that the 'o' in 'not' has been removed.

These forms Always have an Apostrophe

1) If any letters have been removed when a shortened word is made, you'll definitely need an apostrophe.

2) Here's a list of common ones — they're well worth learning:

Long form	Short form		Long form	Short form
I am	I'm		they are	they're
I would	I'd		who is	who's
I had	I'd		do not	don't
I have	I've		does not	doesn't
will not	won't		cannot	can't

3) It can be tricky to remember the difference between 'lets' and 'let's'.

Let's try the cabbage. → *'Let's' is the shortened form of 'let us'. If the sentence makes sense with the long form then you need an apostrophe.*

She lets him try it first. → *'Lets' means 'allows'. It doesn't need an apostrophe.*

Don't let the apostro-flea bite back...

An appropriately-used apostrophe here and there will show the examiner that you're really at the top of your punctuation game. Whatever you do, don't use apostrophes for plurals — "twelve apple's" is just plain wrong.

Possessive Apostrophes

There's one simple rule to learn on this page, but there's an important exception to it too. Sorry about that. As a reward for remembering how to use possessive apostrophes, you'll receive SPaG marks galore.

Use an Apostrophe and '-s' to show Ownership

1) Add an <u>apostrophe</u> and '<u>-s</u>' to <u>nouns</u> to show possession:

The agencys money ran out. ✗

This is wrong — it could lose you marks.

The agency's money ran out. ✓

The apostrophe shows that the money belongs to the agency.

2) If the word is <u>singlar</u> and <u>ends in 's'</u>, you still add an apostrophe and '-s':

Mr Jones's farm is full of weeds.

The walrus's food was stolen.

Add an Apostrophe to most Plural Nouns

1) If the noun is <u>plural</u> and <u>doesn't end in 's'</u>, follow the normal rule and add an <u>apostrophe and 's'</u>:

Many people feel strongly about women's rights.

The rights belong to more than one woman, and the noun doesn't end in 's', so this is the correct ending.

2) But, if a <u>plural noun</u> already <u>ends in 's'</u>, just add an <u>apostrophe</u> to the end:

The plants' ecosystem

The Birlings' reputation

This shows that you're talking about more than one member of the Birling family.

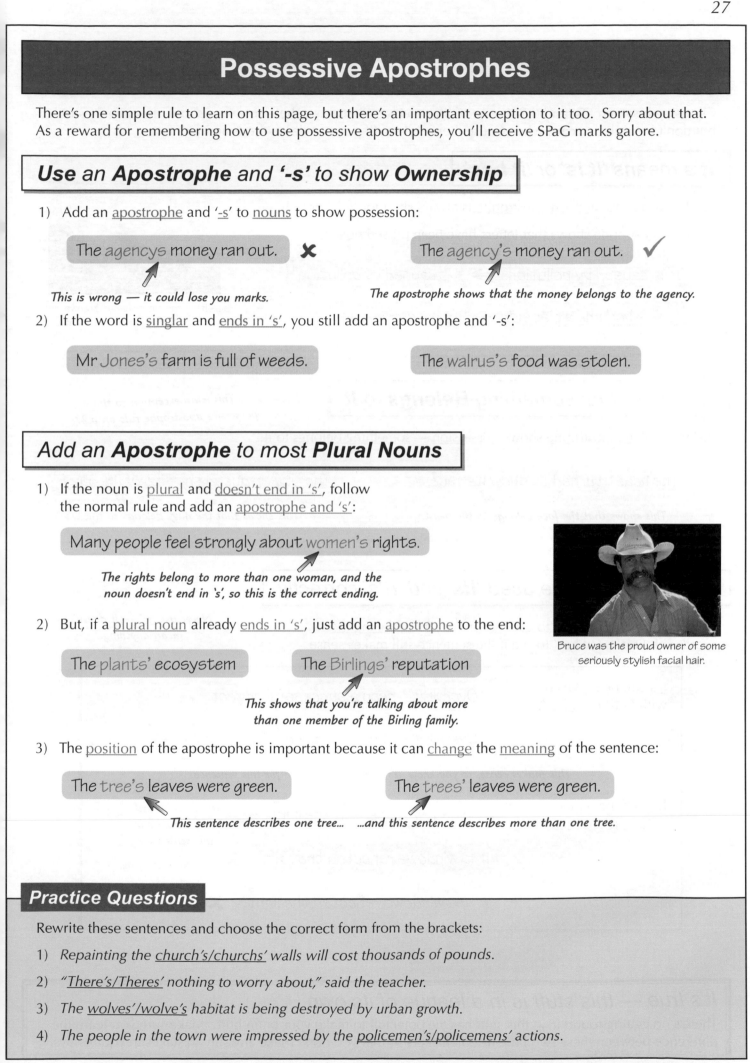

Bruce was the proud owner of some seriously stylish facial hair.

3) The <u>position</u> of the apostrophe is important because it can <u>change</u> the <u>meaning</u> of the sentence:

The tree's leaves were green.

The trees' leaves were green.

This sentence describes one tree...   *...and this sentence describes more than one tree.*

Practice Questions

Rewrite these sentences and choose the correct form from the brackets:

1) *Repainting the <u>church's/churchs'</u> walls will cost thousands of pounds.*

2) *"<u>There's/Theres'</u> nothing to worry about," said the teacher.*

3) *The <u>wolves'/wolve's</u> habitat is being destroyed by urban growth.*

4) *The people in the town were impressed by the <u>policemen's/policemens'</u> actions.*

'Its' and 'It's'

Choosing between 'its' and 'it's' is one of life's eternal dilemmas. These tiny words look deceptively similar, but don't be fooled. Learn when to use them and you'll put a smile on the examiner's face.

It's means '*it is*' or '*it has*'

1) The word 'it's' <u>with an apostrophe</u> is always short for '<u>it is</u>' or '<u>it has</u>'.

2) The <u>apostrophe</u> shows that letters have been <u>missed out</u>.

It is caused by pollution. ⟶ It's caused by pollution.

It has become a classic. ⟶ It's become a classic.

Hamish hoped that he hadn't thrown away marks by forgetting to check his apostrophes.

Its shows that something **Belongs** to **It**

This is an exception to the possessive apostrophe rule on p.27.

'Its' <u>without an apostrophe</u> shows <u>possession</u> — <u>something belongs</u> to <u>it</u>.

The beast turned to show its face.

This shows that the face belongs to the beast.

The USA reduced the size of its navy.

This shows that the navy belongs to the USA.

Check that you've used '*Its*' and '*It's*' correctly

If you're <u>not sure</u> whether to use '<u>its</u>' or '<u>it's</u>', try <u>replacing the word</u> with 'it is' or 'it has' to see if the sentence still makes sense.

Never use <u>its'</u> — it doesn't mean anything.

It's can be replaced with '<u>it is</u>' or '<u>it has</u>':

Overall, it's been a successful project.

Overall, it has been a successful project. ✓

This makes sense, so you know 'it's' is the right option for this sentence.

Its <u>can't</u> be replaced with '<u>it is</u>' or '<u>it has</u>':

Its windows reflected the light.

'Its' doesn't need an apostrophe in this sentence.

It is windows reflected the light. ✗

It has windows reflected the light. ✗

It's true — this stuff is in a league of its own...

There's no getting round it — this stuff has the potential to make your brain hurt. Make sure you learn the difference between these two little troublemakers so that you don't make any silly mistakes in your essays.

Speech Marks

You need to learn how to use speech marks before you can quote in your essays — that's just the way things go. This stuff isn't too scary though, so you'll get the hang of it in no time.

Speech Marks show that someone is Speaking

1) Speech marks go around the actual words that someone says.

> "What should we do about the rumours?" asked Arthur.

Speech marks go at the start and end of the speech.

This is direct speech — it tells you what Arthur actually said.

2) You should only use speech marks if you quote exactly what someone has said.

> Arthur asked what they should do about the rumours.

There's no actual speech in this sentence, so you don't need speech marks.

This is called indirect or reported speech — you don't know exactly what was said.

Speech always ends with a Punctuation Mark

1) Speech always begins with a capital letter, even if it starts in the middle of a sentence.

> Brian complained, "This play doesn't have a happy ending."

2) Speech ends with either a comma, full stop, exclamation mark or question mark. These usually go inside the second set of speech marks.

Use a comma if the sentence continues after the speech ends.
→ "Tell me more," said the Inspector.

Use a full stop if the sentence ends when the speech ends.
→ The President promised, "We'll send supplies."

A comma introduces the speech... ...and a full stop completes it.

Use an exclamation mark if the speech shows strong feelings.
→ "Let's rebel!" shouted the animals.

The exclamation mark means you don't need a comma to separate the speech from the rest of the sentence.

Use a question mark if the speech is a question.
→ Pip asked, "What's the problem?"

3) If the punctuation doesn't belong to the quotation, it goes outside the speech marks.

> Did she really say, "It's mine"?

The question mark belongs to the main sentence, not the quotation so it stays outside the speech marks.

Practice Questions

Rewrite these sentences using either 'it's' or 'its':

1) *The soil had nutrients, but _____ top layer was thin.*

2) *Sometimes _____ difficult to understand poetry.*

3) *Look for the symbols on _____ walls.*

4) *I think _____ been snowing heavily.*

Quoting

Now that you've mastered the art of speech marks, you can move on to the really good stuff — quoting. Quoting from texts or sources is a great way of supporting your argument, as long as you do it right.

Quoting is all about *Backing Up* your *Points*

1) Sometimes you'll need to <u>choose</u> a <u>small part</u> of a text to <u>back up</u> an argument or give as <u>evidence</u> in an essay.

2) It's best to keep your quotes <u>short and snappy</u> — just include the <u>most important bits</u>.

3) Don't forget to use <u>exactly the same</u> words from the original text and copy across any <u>punctuation</u> or <u>capital letters</u>.

4) A quote <u>on its own won't</u> get you any marks — you need to explain <u>why</u> or <u>how</u> it supports the point you're making.

Quotes make any argument more effective.

Quoting from *Novels* or *Articles*

1) Quotes from any text need to be put <u>inside speech marks</u>. If you're just quoting a <u>couple of words</u> try to <u>include</u> them in the middle of your sentence:

> According to the article, the rainforest is being cut down "at an alarming rate".

This quote doesn't interrupt the flow of the sentence.

2) <u>Introduce longer quotes</u> with a colon:

The colon separates the quote from the rest of the sentence.

> The Bible teaches that putting wealth above God is a bad thing: "the love of money is a root of all kinds of evil" (1 Timothy 6:10).

This shows where in the Bible the quote is from — the book, chapter and verse.

Quoting from *Poems*

1) Write <u>short quotes</u> from poems as part of your sentence:

> In 'Quickdraw', the words "trigger of my tongue" sound aggressive.

2) Show where the <u>line endings</u> are for longer quotes:

The colon introduces the quote.

> 'The Farmer's Bride' uses rhyming couplets to give a song-like effect, such as: "We caught her, fetched her home at last / And turned the key upon her, fast".

Use a '/' to show where a new line in the poem begins.

3) Keep the <u>punctuation</u> the same. If the quote comes from the <u>beginning of a line</u>, it usually has a <u>capital letter</u> and if it's from the <u>end</u> of a line, you will have to include any <u>commas</u> or <u>full stops</u>.

"A quote, a quote, my kingdom for a quote..."

Quoting can make all the difference to your essays as long as you choose the words wisely, copy them out correctly, use the right punctuation and add a nifty explanation. Phew, not much to remember then...

Quoting

Quoting from Plays

1) If you're quoting from a play which is in <u>verse</u> and your quote is <u>longer</u> than the line, you need to show where the <u>new line</u> starts.

Large parts of Shakespeare's plays are in verse.

> Capulet thinks that Juliet will be "rul'd / In all respects" by him.

2) If the play <u>isn't in verse</u>, you <u>don't</u> need to show the <u>line endings</u> when you quote.

3) If you're quoting <u>more than a couple of lines</u> or a <u>conversation</u>, you'll need to copy it out exactly as it is written in the play:

Add a little explanation to put the quote in context.

> Romeo and Juliet use religious imagery to talk about love:
>
> Juliet: Saints do not move, though grant for prayers' sake.
> Romeo: Then move not while my prayer's effect I take.
>   Thus from my lips, by thine my sin is purg'd.
>
>   Act 1, Scene 5, lines 105-107

Write the characters' names here.

Show where the quote comes from.

You need to show **Where** the quote **Comes From**

You need to copy the title of the text <u>exactly</u> as it's written, and put it in <u>single quote marks</u>. Try to be <u>specific</u> about where in the text the quote is from.

> For <u>novels</u>, write the chapter (if the novel has chapters):
>
> > In chapter 3 , Darcy insults Elizabeth Bennet.
>
> For <u>poems</u>, write the full name of the poem:
>
> > In 'The Falling Leaves', the poet uses natural imagery to describe dying soldiers.
>
> *Use single quote marks for the title of the poem.*
>
> For <u>plays</u>, write the <u>act</u> and <u>scene</u>:
>
> > Lady Macbeth compares herself to men in Act 1, Scene 5.

Practice Questions

For each of these, write a short passage which includes:

1) *a short quote from a novel.*

2) *a quote of more than one line from a poem.*

3) *a short conversation quoted from a play.*

4) *a quote from a newspaper article.*

Pronouns

It's better to use pronouns in your work rather than using the same nouns over and over again. Examiners hate it when you repeat yourself. Examiners hate it when you repeat yourself. Examiners hate it wh... Oh.

Pronouns take the Place of Nouns

1) <u>Pronouns</u> are words that can be used instead of <u>nouns</u> so you don't keep using the <u>same words</u>.

> Napoleon changes the commandments because Napoleon wants to keep control.

> Napoleon changes the commandments because he wants to keep control.

'He' is a pronoun that replaces the noun 'Napoleon'.

2) The second example sounds more <u>natural</u> because you're not <u>repeating</u> yourself.

Pronouns Change Depending on Function

1) Pronouns <u>change</u> depending on their <u>function</u> in a sentence
   — whether they are <u>doing</u> the action or <u>receiving</u> the action.

> I helped him
doing   *receiving*

> He helped me
doing   *receiving*

2) Pronouns can also show <u>possession</u>.

> This homework is mine
This is who owns the homework.

> These notes are his
This is who owns the notes.

Pronouns also Change Depending on the Number of People

1) Pronouns also <u>change</u> depending on <u>how many people</u> you're talking about.

2) If you're talking about <u>one person</u> or <u>thing</u>, use a <u>singular pronoun</u>.

3) If you're talking about <u>two</u> or <u>more people</u> or <u>things</u>, use a <u>plural pronoun</u>.

SINGULAR PRONOUNS					PLURAL PRONOUNS		
doing	receiving	possession			doing	receiving	possession
I	me	mine / my	1st person		we	us	our / ours
you	you	your / yours	2nd person		you	you	your
he	him	his	3rd person		they	them	their / theirs
she	her	hers					
it	it	its					

Use 'it' for things that aren't people.

When our teacher asked us to name two pronouns, I replied "Who, me?"
You use pronouns all the time, so the stuff on this page is important. Make sure you know what a pronoun is and how it changes in different sentences — once you've understood that, you'll find pronouns a breeze.

Pronouns

Avoid using Too Many pronouns

1) If you use <u>too many</u> pronouns it'll make your writing <u>confusing</u> for the reader.

2) Make it <u>clear</u> at the <u>start</u> of a sentence <u>what</u> the pronouns are <u>referring to</u>:

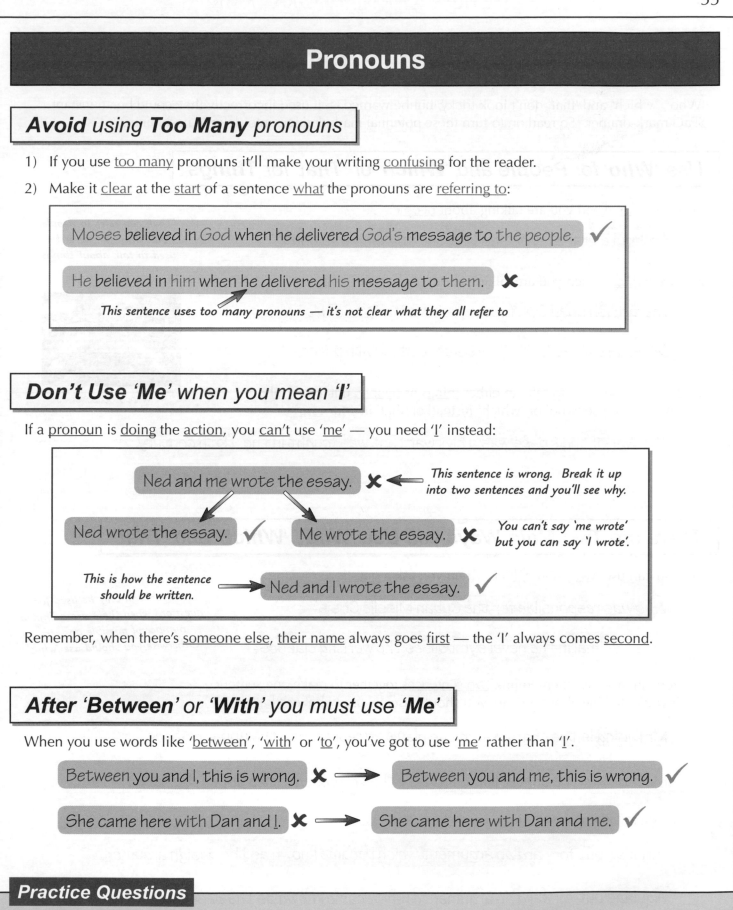

Moses believed in God when he delivered God's message to the people. ✓

He believed in him when he delivered his message to them. ✗

This sentence uses too many pronouns — it's not clear what they all refer to

Don't Use 'Me' when you mean 'I'

If a <u>pronoun</u> is <u>doing</u> the <u>action</u>, you <u>can't</u> use '<u>me</u>' — you need '<u>I</u>' instead:

Ned and me wrote the essay. ✗ ← *This sentence is wrong. Break it up into two sentences and you'll see why.*

Ned wrote the essay. ✓   Me wrote the essay. ✗ *You can't say 'me wrote' but you can say 'I wrote'.*

This is how the sentence should be written. → Ned and I wrote the essay. ✓

Remember, when there's <u>someone else</u>, <u>their name</u> always goes <u>first</u> — the 'I' always comes <u>second</u>.

After 'Between' or 'With' you must use 'Me'

When you use words like '<u>between</u>', '<u>with</u>' or '<u>to</u>', you've got to use '<u>me</u>' rather than '<u>I</u>'.

Between you and I, this is wrong. ✗ ⟶ Between you and me, this is wrong. ✓

She came here with Dan and I. ✗ ⟶ She came here with Dan and me. ✓

Practice Questions

Rewrite these sentences by replacing the underlined words with the correct pronoun from each set of brackets.

1) *Cyclone Nargis was devastating; <u>Cyclone Nargis</u> (it/their/its) path of destruction left people short of food.*

2) *Stalin made the US go to war, which made <u>the US</u> (theirs/them/they) realise <u>Stalin</u> (him/he/his) was a threat.*

3) *Catholics think the Pope is infallible; <u>Catholics</u> (we/they/you) believe <u>the Pope</u> (he/him/you) represents God.*

4) *Lady Macbeth planned to kill Duncan, but <u>Lady Macbeth</u> (she/her/it) didn't kill <u>Duncan</u> (he/his/him) herself.*

Who, Which and That

'Who', 'which' and 'that' don't look tricky, but be warned — if used incorrectly they could be an instant SPaG mark-drainer. So read on to turn these potential mark-drainers into definite no-brainers.

Use 'Who' for People and 'Which' or 'That' for Things

1) Use '<u>who</u>' when you are talking about <u>people</u>:

> Archduke Franz Ferdinand was the man who was shot.

'That' can refer to people, but 'who' can never be used to talk about things.

2) Use '<u>which</u>' when you are talking about <u>animals</u> or <u>things</u>:

> The British used Spitfires, which were a type of plane.

> Doves are animals which are associated with peace.

Whooooooooooo!

3) You can use '<u>that</u>' to refer to either <u>things</u> or <u>people</u>, but if in <u>doubt</u>, you should use 'who' or 'which' <u>instead</u> of 'that' in your <u>essays</u>.

> The War of the Roses was a civil war that was fought in the 15th century.

There are Two Main Ways you Use 'Who', 'Which' and 'That'

1) You can use '<u>who</u>' and '<u>which</u>' when you ask a <u>question</u>.

> Who was responsible for the Cuban Missile Crisis?

> Which animal in the novel symbolises the working classes?

'Which' can only be used for questions when there are a limited number of possible answers. Otherwise you should use 'what'.

2) You can also use them to <u>link two sentences</u> together to <u>make one sentence</u>. If you're talking about <u>people</u>, you should <u>usually</u> use '<u>who</u>' or '<u>that</u>'.

> Mr Birling is the character in the play who represents the upper classes.

> Mr Birling is the character in the play that represents the upper classes.

If you're talking about things, use '<u>which</u>' and '<u>that</u>'.

> Aquinas put forward an argument which became known as the design argument.

> Aquinas put forward an argument that became known as the design argument.

"I'm Barney the barn owl" "Twit T-who?" "I think you mean Twit T-which..."

'Who', 'which' and 'that' are incredibly useful little words. Remember, 'who' goes with people, but 'which' and 'that' usually go with animals and things. Some people act like animals but they still need a 'who'.

Who or Whom, Who's or Whose

These words are all variations of 'who', so you can only use them to refer to people — simple. However, when to use each one can get you in a pickle. This page should be a handy guide to put you in the know.

'Who' is the **Subject** of a sentence, 'Whom' is the **Object**

For a reminder of 'doing' and 'receiving' pronouns, see p.32.

1) If the person you're talking about is the subject (doing the action) — use 'who'.

> Seismologists are people who study earthquakes.

'who' is the subject, 'earthquakes' is the object.

2) If the person you're talking about is the object (receiving the action)— use 'whom'.

Eva Smith is receiving sympathy — so you need the object form 'whom'.

> Eva Smith is a character whom everyone can sympathise with.

3) Check which pronoun to use by replacing 'who' or 'whom' with another pronoun. If the 'doing' pronoun (he, she or they) makes sense, use 'who'. If the receiving pronoun (him, her or them) works, use 'whom'.

> Seismologists are people. They study earthquakes. ✓

> Them study earthquakes. ✗

Separate the sentence into clauses, then replace the pronoun. 'Seismologists' is plural so you need to use 'they' or 'them'.

'They study earthquakes' makes sense so 'who' must be right.

With trickier sentences, you might need to reorganise the sentence when you replace the pronoun.

> Eva Smith is a character. She everyone can sympathise with.

This is nonsense — so try switching the order about.

> Everyone can sympathise with she. ✗

> Everyone can sympathise with her. ✓

'... sympathise with she' is wrong — it should be '... sympathise with her', so 'whom' is correct.

'Who's' means 'Who Is' but 'Whose' is **Possessive**

1) 'Who's' is the shortened form of 'who is' or 'who has'.

> Who's got the most lines in the play?

This means 'who has got the most lines...'

> Romeo is the character who's most vocal.

This means '... the character who is most vocal.'

2) If you want to say 'belonging to whom' you need to use 'whose'.

> Whose essay is this?

This means 'to whom does the essay belong?'

Practice Questions

Rewrite these sentences using the correct underlined word so that they make sense.

1) *Wordsworth is one of the authors whom/who we can thank for the birth of Romanticism.*

2) *There is still debate over whose/who's responsible for the assassination of President Kennedy.*

3) *One campaigner which/who is very famous is Martin Luther King, who's/whose words inspired thousands.*

4) *The Pope, who's/whose the leader of the Catholic church, said which/that contraception is immoral.*

Verbs

Learning about verbs is about as exciting as eating your greens. But unlike eating your greens, learning about verbs won't make you grow up big and strong. However, it could help you snag some tasty SPaG marks.

Verbs are *'Doing'* or *'Being'* Words

There are two types of verb — 'doing' verbs, which describe an action, and 'being' verbs, which describe a state of being.

Every sentence has to have a verb.

Dickens uses alliteration. ⟵ *The verb is 'uses'.*

This is a 'doing' word — 'doing' words tell you what happens.

The novel is controversial. ⟵ *The verb is 'is'.*

This is a 'being' word — 'being' words tell you how something is.

Verbs must always **Agree** with their **Subjects**

1) Verbs need to agree with their subject (the person or thing doing the action). If they don't agree, the sentence won't make sense.

2) Some verbs change depending on their subject. Singular subjects need a singular form of the verb, and plural subjects need a plural form of the verb.

The 'volcanologist' is the subject because he is 'doing' the action. 'Volcanologist' is singular, as it's only one person.

The subject here is 'Volcanologists' — there's more than one person, so this is plural.

A volcanologist studies volcanoes.

Volcanologists study volcanoes.

'studies' is the verb. It's singular.

The verb 'study' is plural to match the subject.

The **Tense** of a verb tells you **When** it **Happens**

Verbs can be in the past tense, the present tense or the future tense.

Stalin ruled all of Russia. ⟵ *past tense* ⟹ Stalin has ruled all of Russia.

Stalin rules all of Russia. ⟵ *present tense* ⟹ Stalin is ruling all of Russia.

Stalin will rule all of Russia. ⟵ *future tense* ⟹ Stalin will be ruling all of Russia.

Learning about verbs makes me feel really tense...

Verbs are crucial — without them, you wouldn't have a sentence that makes any sense. What you really need to know is that verbs always agree with their subject, and sometimes that means a change in spelling.

Forming the Present Tense

The problem with the present tense is that people think it's easy and end up making silly mistakes. There's only one way to avoid that — you'll have to learn how to form it properly.

Regular Verbs follow a Pattern in the Present

1) The <u>present</u> tense is easy to form — <u>most</u> of the <u>regular verbs</u> don't change at all. The verb only <u>changes</u> when the subject is <u>he</u>, <u>she</u> or <u>it</u>. Then you have to <u>add an 's'</u> to the end of the verb.

Remember to add an 's' to the end of verbs where the subject is 'he', 'she' or 'it' — these are third person singular pronouns.

2) Some nouns like 'family', 'audience' or 'government' are <u>singular</u> even though they refer to <u>more than one</u> person. Make sure you use the <u>third person singular</u> form of the verb.

The audience stands near the stage.   The jury gives its verdict.

The words 'jury' and 'audience' are singular so you need the third person singular form of the verb (this is the form you would use if 'the jury' was replaced by the pronouns 'he', 'she' or 'it').

You need to Know these Irregular Forms

1) A <u>lot</u> of verbs <u>don't</u> follow the <u>regular present tense pattern</u> — these are called <u>irregular verbs</u>.

2) Here are two of the <u>most common</u> ones. There's <u>no trick</u> to them — you'll just have to <u>learn</u> them.

Verb	I	You (sg.)	He	She	It	We	You (pl.)	They
to be	am	are	is	is	is	are	are	are
to have	have	have	has	has	has	have	have	have

3) Some verbs are <u>slightly irregular</u> — you need to do <u>more</u> to them than just add 's' when the subject is '<u>he</u>', '<u>she</u>' or '<u>it</u>'.

4) If the verb ends in a <u>vowel</u> or a <u>consonant and y</u>, you need to add '<u>es</u>' to the end of the verb.

he flies   it does   she goes

Remember, the 'y' changes to an 'i'.

Practice Questions

Change the verbs in brackets so that the sentences below are in the present tense.

1) *She (to go) to every play that she can. It (to be) a time-consuming hobby, but I (to think) it's worth it.*

2) *You (to try) very hard to get good marks. I (to hope) that I (to revise) enough to do just as well.*

3) *My brother and I (to be) interested in physics. He often (to fly) his kite to study the effect of gravity.*

4) *My teacher (to tell) us that the novel (to take) some understanding, but its message (to be) important.*

Section Three — Grammar

Forming -ing Verbs

A really useful little grammar gem is the '-ing' form. You can use it to describe actions that haven't been completed in the present or the past. Use it correctly to unlock ninety free bonus points (no cash value).

The -ing Verb says what Is or Was Happening

1) When you want to talk about <u>action</u> that <u>is still happening</u>, or <u>was happening</u> in the past, you need to use the <u>present</u> or <u>past</u> form of the verb 'to be' plus the <u>main verb</u> in its '<u>-ing</u>' form.

2) So, if you're writing in the present tense, you'll need either '<u>am</u>', '<u>are</u>' or '<u>is</u>'. If you're writing in the past tense, use '<u>was</u>' or '<u>were</u>'.

3) Then the <u>main verb</u> adds '<u>-ing</u>' on the end.

Main verbs are the most important verbs in a phrase.

4) Here's how to change '<u>I think</u>' into the '-ing' form:

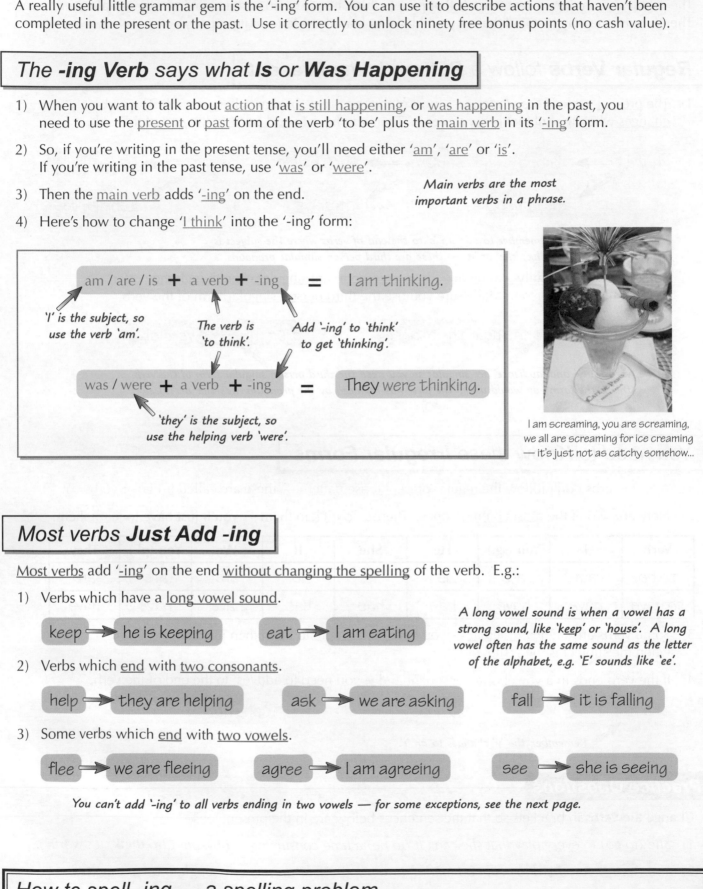

'I' is the subject, so use the verb 'am'.

The verb is 'to think'.

Add '-ing' to 'think' to get 'thinking'.

'they' is the subject, so use the helping verb 'were'.

I am screaming, you are screaming, we all are screaming for ice creaming — it's just not as catchy somehow...

Most verbs Just Add -ing

<u>Most verbs</u> add '<u>-ing</u>' on the end <u>without changing the spelling</u> of the verb. E.g.:

1) Verbs which have a <u>long vowel sound</u>.

keep ⟶ he is keeping   eat ⟶ I am eating

A long vowel sound is when a vowel has a strong sound, like 'keep' or 'house'. A long vowel often has the same sound as the letter of the alphabet, e.g. 'E' sounds like 'ee'.

2) Verbs which <u>end</u> with <u>two consonants</u>.

help ⟶ they are helping   ask ⟶ we are asking   fall ⟶ it is falling

3) Some verbs which <u>end</u> with <u>two vowels</u>.

flee ⟶ we are fleeing   agree ⟶ I am agreeing   see ⟶ she is seeing

You can't add '-ing' to all verbs ending in two vowels — for some exceptions, see the next page.

How to spell -ing — a spelling problem...

A nice easy rule to learn here. Don't forget — you need to use the right form of 'to be' + verb + -ing to form this tense. You probably use '-ing' forms all the time, so there's no excuse for not using them perfectly.

Spelling -ing Verbs

All the stuff about -ing words has been pretty easy so far — but here's where it gets tough. Some verbs are a nightmare to spell because you have to add letters or take them away. Learn these rules right now.

Some words *Double* the *Final Consonant*

1) For short verbs with <u>short vowel sounds</u> which <u>end</u> in a <u>single consonant</u> you need to <u>double the final consonant</u> (unless it's an 'x') before adding '-ing'.

Short vowels are any vowel sounds which are not long vowels e.g. 'a' in 'apple', or 'i' in 'pit'.

to flap

'Flap' has the short vowel sound 'a', and it ends in a consonant — 'p'.

flapping

You need to double the 'p' and then add '-ing'.

2) Some <u>longer verbs</u> also follow this <u>pattern</u> — if the verb has <u>two</u> or <u>more syllables</u>, work out which syllable is <u>stressed</u>. A stressed syllable is the <u>part</u> of the <u>word</u> that you say with <u>more emphasis</u>.

A syllable is a word, or part of a word, which can be said in a single sound, e.g. 'beauty' has two syllables, 'beau' and 'ty'.

3) If the <u>first</u> syllable is <u>stressed</u>, just <u>add '-ing'</u>.

visiting

4) If the <u>second</u> syllable is <u>stressed</u>, <u>double</u> the <u>consonant</u> before <u>adding '-ing'</u>.

preferring

When you say 'prefer', you put more stress on the second syllable, 'fer'. So you need to double the final consonant before adding -ing.

5) There are some <u>exceptions</u> where words <u>end</u> in an <u>unstressed syllable</u>, but the consonant is still <u>doubled</u>.

An exception is any word ending with an unstressed syllable and 'l' — in this case the 'l' is doubled.

levelling

Some verbs Drop *the* Final *'e' before adding* -ing

1) Verbs with a <u>silent 'e'</u> at the end drop the 'e' before adding '-ing'.

A silent 'e' is one which you don't hear, e.g. the 'e' at the end of 'bite'.

to take → taking

'Take' ends in a silent 'e'.

You need to remove the 'e' before adding '-ing'.

2) Most <u>verbs</u> which <u>end</u> in '<u>ie</u>' drop the 'e' and <u>change</u> the 'i' to 'y'.

tie → tying   die → dying   lie → lying

Practice Questions

Change these present tense verbs into -ing verbs.

1) buy
2) clap
3) wait
4) dance
5) shake
6) lie
7) dig
8) drive
9) get
10) brake
11) win
12) begin

Section Three — Grammar

The Simple Past

The past tense is like the present tense, except it talks about things that have already happened. People are always getting past tense verbs in a tangle. You need to learn this page to stay out of trouble.

Regular Verbs add '-ed' to form the Simple Past

'-ed' is a suffix so it follows the spelling rules on p.4.

1) Lots of verbs form the <u>simple past</u> by <u>adding</u> '<u>-ed</u>' to the <u>end</u>.

work → worked   hope → hoped   study → studied

Verbs ending in 'e' just add '-d' on the end to form the simple past tense.

Verbs ending in 'y' usually change the 'y' to 'i' before adding the '-ed' ending.

2) The rule for verbs of <u>two or more syllables</u> is slightly different. You might need to <u>double</u> the <u>final consonant</u> if the final syllable is stressed.

3) You can follow the <u>rules on p.39</u> for doubling consonants when adding '-ed'.

admit → admitted   occur → occurred   cover → covered

The stressed syllable is at the end of the word, so double the consonant.

The syllable at the end of the word isn't stressed so you just add '-ed'.

Some Irregular verbs you need to Learn

1) Not all verbs add '-ed' — lots of verbs in the simple past tense are <u>irregular</u>. Here are some common ones.

Verbs	The Simple Past	Verbs	The Simple Past	Verbs	The Simple Past
to do	did	to get	got	to make	made
to have	had	to wear	wore	to fight	fought
to see	saw	to be	was / were	to come	came
to sleep	slept	to go	went	to eat	ate
to think	thought	to take	took	to steal	stole

2) Some verbs <u>don't change at all</u> in the simple past tense.

cut → I cut my finger yesterday. ✓   I cutted my finger yesterday. ✗

This is wrong and will lose you marks.

3) Here are some of the most <u>common examples</u>:

put   beat   hurt   cost   hit   cut   set   let

Learning grammar on a farm — 'I have dung'...

Phew — it all seems a bit tricky. Always make sure that you've formed the past tense correctly. It's unfortunate that lots of really common words are irregular, so it's worth spending some extra time on those.

The Past Tense with 'Have'

There's another way to talk about something that happened in the past — it's the past tense with 'have'. It has a slightly different meaning to the simple past, as you're about to find out. Lucky you...

It's *Different* to the *Simple Past*

1) The <u>past tense</u> with '<u>have</u>' describes something that happened <u>recently</u> but that has <u>finished</u> now.

2) You'll also see it used to describe something that has been <u>going on</u> for a <u>period</u> of time.

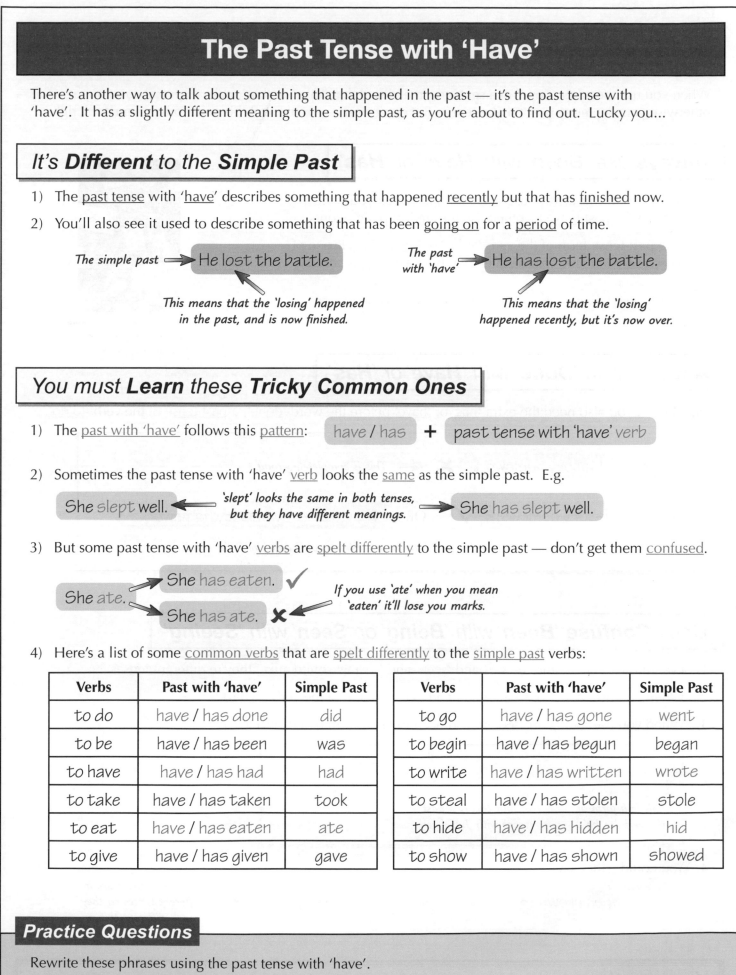

The simple past → He lost the battle.

This means that the 'losing' happened in the past, and is now finished.

The past with 'have' → He has lost the battle.

This means that the 'losing' happened recently, but it's now over.

You must *Learn* these *Tricky Common Ones*

1) The <u>past with 'have'</u> follows this <u>pattern</u>: have / has **+** past tense with 'have' verb

2) Sometimes the past tense with 'have' <u>verb</u> looks the <u>same</u> as the simple past. E.g.

She slept well. ← *'slept' looks the same in both tenses, but they have different meanings.* → She has slept well.

3) But some past tense with 'have' <u>verbs</u> are <u>spelt differently</u> to the simple past — don't get them <u>confused</u>.

She ate. → She has eaten. ✓
→ She has ate. ✗ ← *If you use 'ate' when you mean 'eaten' it'll lose you marks.*

4) Here's a list of some <u>common verbs</u> that are <u>spelt differently</u> to the <u>simple past</u> verbs:

Verbs	Past with 'have'	Simple Past
to do	have / has done	did
to be	have / has been	was
to have	have / has had	had
to take	have / has taken	took
to eat	have / has eaten	ate
to give	have / has given	gave

Verbs	Past with 'have'	Simple Past
to go	have / has gone	went
to begin	have / has begun	began
to write	have / has written	wrote
to steal	have / has stolen	stole
to hide	have / has hidden	hid
to show	have / has shown	showed

Practice Questions

Rewrite these phrases using the past tense with 'have'.

1) *He begins*
2) *It hides*
3) *They do*
4) *We have*
5) *We visit*
6) *She steals*
7) *It eats*
8) *It breaks*

The Past Tense with 'Have'

When you use 'been' or 'done' in a sentence, make sure that 'have' or 'has' make a special guest appearance — otherwise your sentence won't make sense. But don't worry — you've got this page to help you get it right.

Always use *'Been'* with *'Have'* or *'Has'*

1) Some verb forms always use 'have' or 'has' when you write them in the past tense — otherwise they're just plain wrong.

2) One past tense form of the verb 'to be' is 'been'. This is one of those awkward verb forms which needs an extra 'have' or 'has'.

I been writing. ✗   I have been writing. ✓

I have been, I have asparagus, I have spinach — anything your heart desires...

Always write *'Done'* with *'Have'* or *'Has'*

Like 'been', you also need the extra 'has' or 'have' before the word 'done', a past tense of the verb 'to do'.

I done my history homework. ✗ ⬅ *This is completely wrong.*

I did my history homework. ✓   OR   I have done my history homework. ✓

You can only write 'I did' or 'I have done'. Never put 'I done', or 'I have did'.

Don't **Confuse** *'Been'* with *'Being'* or *'Seen'* with *'Seeing'*

1) Even though 'been' and 'being', and 'seen' and 'seeing' sound alike, they're different tenses.

2) When you use 'been' or 'seen' you need to use a form of the verb 'to have'.

3) When you use 'being' or 'seeing' you need to use a form of the verb 'to be'.

He was been crowned. ✗ ⬅ *This is wrong and will lose you marks.*

This is a form of the verb 'to be'...   *...but this is a past tense with 'have' verb.*

4) You could either say:

He has been crowned. ✓ *or* He was being crowned. ✓ ⬅ *These sentences are in different tenses so they mean different things.*

You have been revising — you deserve a treat...

The past tense with 'have' could trip you up if you don't know what you're doing. But you won't go far wrong if you remember that 'been' and 'done' always go with 'has' or 'have'. It's a golden grammar rule.

'Have' and 'Of'

One of the main mistakes with 'have' is confusing it with 'of'. They sound pretty similar, especially if you say them ten times quickly. Haveofhavofavofvofvof. Although they sound alike, they don't mean the same thing.

It's easy to **Confuse** 'Have' and 'Of'

1) Have a look at these <u>sentences</u>:

They could of won the battle. ✘   They could have won the battle. ✔

God might of made the choice. ✘   God might have made the choice. ✔

2) 'Could of' and 'might of' both <u>seem right</u> because they <u>sound similar</u> to the shortened versions '<u>could've</u>' and '<u>might've</u>'.

3) However, 'could of' and 'might of' are <u>wrong</u>. If you use them in the <u>exam</u> when you mean 'could have' or 'might have' you'll <u>lose marks</u>.

Don't use shortened versions like 'could've' or 'might've' in your exam — they're too informal.

Use '**Have**', NOT '**Of**'

1) It's easy to get 'could of' and 'could have' <u>muddled</u> — so, remember this golden rule. Whenever you use these <u>verbs</u>, <u>always</u> use '<u>have</u>', <u>never</u> use '<u>of</u>'.

Examiners are really picky about people writing 'of' instead of 'have'. It's worth practising this until you get it right.

- may
- might
- should
- shall
- would
- will
- could
- can
- must

2) If you're confused, remember that '<u>have</u>' is a <u>verb</u> so it follows <u>other doing words</u> e.g.:

...so the rainfall must have been higher.   Romeo could have saved Juliet if he...

3) '<u>Of</u>' is a <u>preposition</u> — you'd use it in phrases such as:

Lots of Muslims believe that...   Historians disagree because of...

Practice Questions

Rewrite the sentences below, correcting them as you go, so that they make perfect sense.

1) *They shouldn't of done that, because it got me into trouble. I might of been given detention.*

2) *You could of helped us finish dessert. We couldn't finish it because of the amount of sugar in it.*

3) *The flooding may of been caused by lots of heavy rain falling on the hills and mountains.*

Negatives

'No' and 'not' are those great little words you use to say that you don't like something or you don't want to do something. Unfortunately, sentences with negatives like these are really easy to get wrong.

Don't use *Double Negatives*

1) <u>Double negatives</u> are when you have <u>two nos</u> or <u>nots</u> in a phrase together. It's a sure-fire way to <u>lose marks</u>, because they <u>don't</u> make any <u>sense</u>.

> I don't like nobody here. ✗ ← *This is wrong — the sentence 'I do not like nobody here' doesn't mean anything.*
>
> I like nobody here. ✓   I don't like anybody here. ✓
> *Here's one correct way to say it...*   *...and here's another — just don't confuse them.*

2) <u>Avoid</u> using the word '<u>no</u>' in phrases with '<u>-n't</u>' or '<u>not</u>'. You should use the word '<u>any</u>' instead.

> We haven't got no milk. ✗   We haven't got any milk. ✓
> *This is wrong...*   *...this is much better.*

3) '<u>None</u>' is <u>another word</u> like '<u>no</u>' — if you use a word ending with '<u>-n't</u>' you shouldn't use another <u>negative</u>.

> I haven't got none. ✗   I haven't got any. ✓
> *None is another word like 'no' that should be treated in the same way.*
>
> *'Nothing' and 'nowhere' are other words like 'no'.*

'Ain't' isn't a proper word — use *'Hasn't'*, *'Isn't'* or *'Haven't'*

Even though <u>loads</u> of people <u>use it</u>, and you might even find it in a <u>dictionary</u>, using 'ain't' in your work is a big <u>mistake</u>.

> It ain't happened yet. ✗   It hasn't happened yet. ✓
>
> It ain't working. ✗   It isn't working. ✓
>
> I ain't done nothing. ✗   I haven't done anything. ✓

If you're not sure which word to use instead of 'ain't', try each one until one of them fits — you'll know when it sounds right.

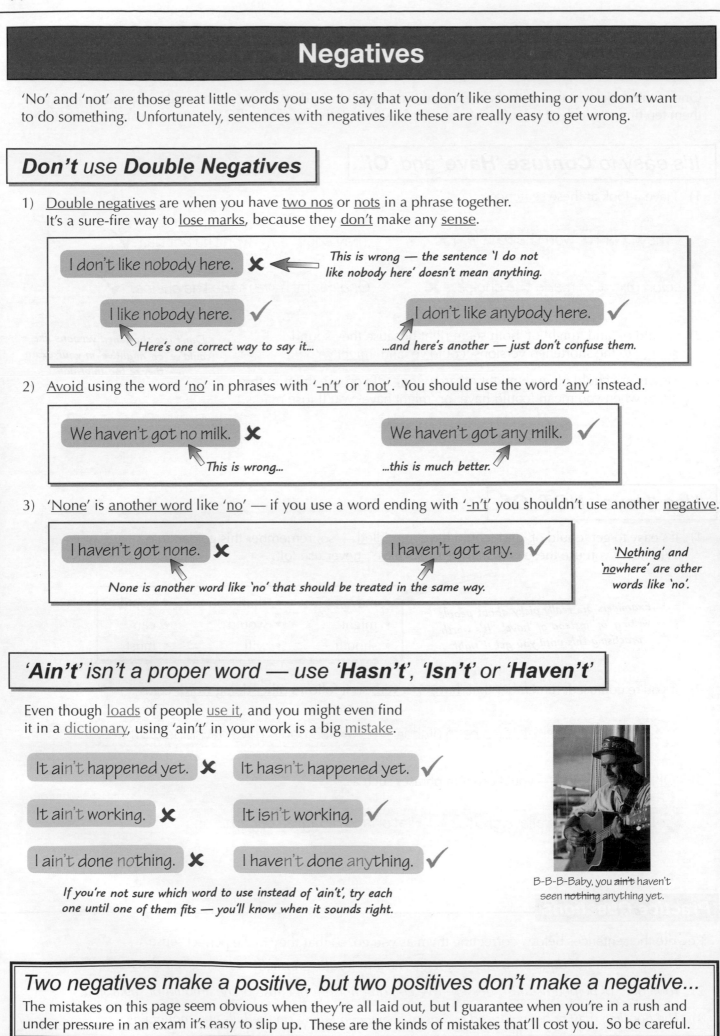

B-B-B-Baby, you ~~ain't~~ haven't seen ~~nothing~~ anything yet.

Two negatives make a positive, but two positives don't make a negative...

The mistakes on this page seem obvious when they're all laid out, but I guarantee when you're in a rush and under pressure in an exam it's easy to slip up. These are the kinds of mistakes that'll cost you. So be careful.

Negatives

This page is all about two negatives — 'don't' and 'doesn't'. If life has taught me anything, it's that two negatives always make a positive. "And what's the positive?" I hear you cry. Lovely, shiny SPaG marks...

Don't = *do not* and *doesn't* = *does not*

1) Use '<u>doesn't</u>' with '<u>he</u>', '<u>she</u>' and '<u>it</u>', or when using the name of <u>just one</u> person or thing. ⟹ The author *doesn't* use a lot of description.

2) Use '<u>don't</u>' if you're writing about <u>more than one</u> person or thing. ⟹ Rivers *don't* all flow at the same speed.

3) Use 'don't' in sentences with '<u>you</u>' or '<u>I</u>'. ⟹ I *don't* believe that this is right.

Use the **long form** to **check** you're right

If you're not sure which one is right, use the <u>long form</u> ('<u>does not</u>' or '<u>do not</u>') to check.

Curley *don't* like Lennie = Curley *do not* like Lennie. ✗

This sounds wrong when you put it in the long form.

Curley *doesn't* like Lennie = Curley *does not* like Lennie. ✓

This sounds right when you put it in the long form.

The farms *doesn't* produce wheat = The farms *does not* produce wheat. ✗

This sounds wrong when you put it in the long form.

The farms *don't* produce wheat = The farms *do not* produce wheat. ✓

This sounds right when you put it in the long form.

Practice Questions

Rewrite these sentences, using either 'don't' or 'doesn't'.

1) *She _____ like me, and her brother _____ like me either.*

2) *I _____ enjoy eating cabbage, but Kitty _____ enjoy eating peas.*

3) *Ella and Kamal _____ have a pet, and I _____ have a bike.*

4) *Frank _____ want to go to the cinema, but you _____ like going on your own.*

Staying in the Right Tense

Switching tenses is the biggest mistake you need to avoid with verbs. That means you've got to learn to use tenses properly. Make sure you don't go mixing up the present with the past and the past with the future.

Don't change tenses in your writing by *Mistake*

Once you've picked a <u>tense</u>, you'll usually need to <u>stick to it</u>. Make sure all the <u>verbs</u> agree with each other.

This is in the past tense.

Another past verb.

> As Ralph tried to put the fire out, he heard distant splashes. Suddenly, he sees a boat.

This one's wrong — it's present when it should be past. The correct verb would be 'saw'.

You stay in the right tense, and we'll have the left tense.

Use *Past Verbs* in *Past Writing*

1) Be consistent — <u>don't switch</u> tenses accidentally. Stay in <u>one tense</u> so it's <u>clear</u> what's going on.

2) If you <u>start</u> writing in the past, you've got to <u>stay</u> in the past.

> The Battle of Hastings was an important turning point in English history. It allowed William II of Normandy to seize the throne, as the English King (Harold II) was killed on the battlefield.

In history essays you should usually use the past tense.

All the verbs here are past forms — you can tell exactly what's going on.

Be *Especially Careful* with the *Present*

You need the <u>present</u> for <u>English literature essays</u>, but don't <u>mix</u> past and present forms by mistake.

> Even though Piggy is annoying, Ralph realised he is his only ally. ✗

'realised' is past tense, but the rest of the sentence is in the present.

> Even though Piggy is annoying, Ralph realises he is his only ally. ✓

This is how the sentence should be written — it's much better because the description is brought to life by using the present.

Consistency of tenses — a sticky business...

Sticking to the same tense — it sounds so simple. But when you're writing in a hurry, it's easy to put the wrong one down without thinking. Learn this page and remember your tenses when you write.

Paragraphs

Paragraphs are horrible things — you know you ought to use them, but they're a big hassle. I know they're a pain to remember, but it's really important you know how to use them so that you can improve your work.

Paragraphs make your writing **Clearer**

1) A paragraph is a <u>group of sentences</u> which talk about the <u>same thing</u>, or <u>follow on</u> from each other.

2) Every time you start a <u>new paragraph</u>, you're showing that <u>something new</u> has happened, or it's a <u>new point</u>.

3) <u>Everything</u> you write <u>must</u> be in <u>paragraphs</u>, or it could <u>cost</u> you — you'll <u>drop marks</u> if you forget them.

The ideas in this paragraph are all related. They're about Boxer's injured hoof.

...but they refused to let him rest.

Boxer desperately tried to keep the pain from his split hoof hidden from the other animals. It was difficult, because he was in such agony, but he realised it was important for morale.

Benjamin knew that the pigs would never let Boxer stop work until he was physically unable to...

These paragraphs talk about something different.

Make the **Beginning** *and* **End** *of each paragraph* **Clear**

You need to make it <u>clear</u> to the examiner where each paragraph <u>starts</u> and <u>finishes</u>.

1) Leave a <u>space</u> on the <u>first line</u>.

2) Leave a <u>gap</u> at the <u>end</u> of the <u>last sentence</u>.

3) Start your new paragraph on a <u>new line</u>.

Remember the space for the next paragraph.

This is a very important rule. Every new paragraph must have a space between the margin and the first word.

Here's how to end a paragraph. Finish the last sentence and leave the rest of that line blank — even if there's a lot of line left.

Leave another space every time you start a new paragraph. This shows you're writing about something different.

Just leave the rest of this line blank.

Practice Questions

Change the underlined verbs so that the tense is consistent in each sentence.

1) *When the birth rate is higher than the death rate, the population of a country <u>grew</u>.*

2) *A 'Holy War' <u>was</u> a war where people believe that God is 'on their side'.*

3) *George <u>has decided</u> to look after Lennie because he feels sorry for him.*

4) *Religion can help to bring families together, but it can also <u>caused</u> conflict.*

Paragraphs

Starting and finishing paragraphs can be a tricky business. One thing's for sure though — if your essay answers are one continuous block of text you can say "bye-bye" to SPaG marks.

There's a **Simple Trick** to **Using Paragraphs Properly**

1) Start a <u>new paragraph</u> every time something <u>changes</u> or if you're making a <u>new point</u>.

2) Don't worry about how <u>long</u> or <u>short</u> your <u>paragraphs</u> are — just make sure they're <u>totally clear</u>.

3) If you <u>forget</u> to start a new paragraph, put a <u>double strike</u> (like this '///') next to where your new paragraph <u>should go</u>.

For more on correcting mistakes see p. 52-53.

"When I talk about something new, I start a new parrot-graph."

When you make a **New Point**

If you're making a <u>new point</u> you need to start a <u>new paragraph</u>.

This paragraph is about the positive results of animal experimentation.

> Some people argue that experimenting on animals is a necessary evil because it has led to the development of various vaccines and cures which have saved millions of lives.
>
> Others believe that there is no justification for animal cruelty, regardless of the benefits...

Don't forget to indent new paragraphs.

This bit is arguing against animal cruelty so it's a new point and needs a new paragraph.

When you talk about a **New Person**

Whenever you talk about a <u>different person</u>, you need a <u>different paragraph</u>.

If you're writing dialogue, you need to start a new line every time someone different starts speaking.

This paragraph is about Mrs Birling.

> Mrs Birling believes that reputation and social status are more important than helping people in need. She uses her "influence" to persuade members of her charity to reject Eva's desperate request for money simply because her pride has been injured.
>
> Gerald Croft also believes in the importance of social status and reputation, but his hypocrisy is perhaps far worse...

Gerald's a new person, so you need a new paragraph.

Don't forget to leave a space before a new paragraph.

Astronauts understand paragraphs — they always leave space behind...

Paragraphs aren't as pointless as you might think. Unless you write in paragraphs, it'll be difficult for the examiner to follow the thread of your answer. And that means you won't get as many SPaG marks.

Paragraphs

When you start writing about a *New Place*

A new place also needs a new paragraph.

This paragraph is about a city in Italy.

> In 2009, an earthquake struck the city of L'Aquila, Italy, that measured 5.8 on the Richter scale. High standards of building construction and well-trained volunteers meant that around 300 people died.
>
> However, in Kashmir, Pakistan, they were completely unprepared for earthquakes, which resulted in around 80 000 deaths.

This needs a new paragraph, because it's talking about somewhere else.

When you *Move* to a *Different Time*

If you're talking about a different time, it's time for a new paragraph.

> There were many significant advances in the field of medicine in the 19th century. For example, X-rays were used for the first time. These allowed doctors to see what was happening inside somebody without having to operate.
>
> Nowadays medicine is advancing so quickly that it seems like anything might one day be possible. Nanorobotics and stem cell research are just a couple of developments that could revolutionise medicine as we know it.

The first paragraph's about the 19th century.

This one's gone forward to a different time — it's about the present.

Practice Questions

Rewrite this piece of text, putting in paragraphs where you think they belong:

Hitler was able to control the lives of German people between 1933 and 1939 by using a range of methods. After 1933 all political parties other than the Nazis were banned. Communist and socialist leaders who stayed in Germany were arrested, and those who could went into exile elsewhere in Europe. The Nazis set up a series of concentration camps for all their political opponents and these were soon used to imprison other groups in society who did not fit in with Hitler's vision of a pure German race. A system soon developed where people could be arrested and questioned without any real cause. Propaganda was also a key factor. The Party controlled all public information and nothing could be broadcast on radio, shown in cinemas or printed in newspapers unless it had been approved. The school system, youth groups and all other cultural activities were all linked to the Nazi propaganda machine.

Checking Your Work

Now that you've got your head around the ins and outs of SPaG, it's time to round off the fun with some exam tips. The last thing you want to do is waste your hard work by making silly mistakes on the big day.

Remember to Check what you've Written

1) Leave <u>5 minutes</u> at the end of the exam to <u>check your work</u>.

2) Check as <u>many</u> questions as you can, but make sure you read over the questions which award <u>SPaG marks</u> especially <u>carefully</u>.

3) 5 minutes <u>isn't</u> long, so there <u>won't</u> be time to check <u>everything</u> thoroughly. Look for the <u>most obvious</u> spelling, punctuation and grammar <u>mistakes</u>.

Don't use the last 5 minutes of the exam to put your feet up and relax.

Watch out for Common Spelling Errors

Check for missing words as well as misspelt words.

When you're writing under pressure, it's <u>easy</u> to let <u>spelling mistakes</u> creep in, but there are a few things you can watch out for:

1) Look out for <u>common homophones</u> — words which <u>sound the same</u> but are <u>spelt differently</u>:

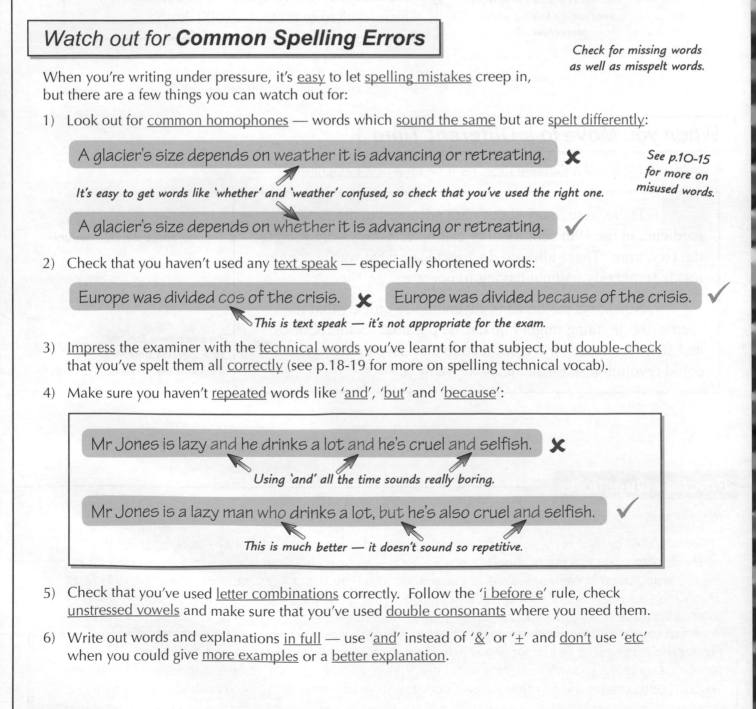

A glacier's size depends on weather it is advancing or retreating. ✗

It's easy to get words like 'whether' and 'weather' confused, so check that you've used the right one.

See p.10-15 for more on misused words.

A glacier's size depends on whether it is advancing or retreating. ✓

2) Check that you haven't used any <u>text speak</u> — especially shortened words:

Europe was divided cos of the crisis. ✗   Europe was divided because of the crisis. ✓

This is text speak — it's not appropriate for the exam.

3) <u>Impress</u> the examiner with the <u>technical words</u> you've learnt for that subject, but <u>double-check</u> that you've spelt them all <u>correctly</u> (see p.18-19 for more on spelling technical vocab).

4) Make sure you haven't <u>repeated</u> words like '<u>and</u>', '<u>but</u>' and '<u>because</u>':

Mr Jones is lazy and he drinks a lot and he's cruel and selfish. ✗

Using 'and' all the time sounds really boring.

Mr Jones is a lazy man who drinks a lot, but he's also cruel and selfish. ✓

This is much better — it doesn't sound so repetitive.

5) Check that you've used <u>letter combinations</u> correctly. Follow the '<u>i before e</u>' rule, check <u>unstressed vowels</u> and make sure that you've used <u>double consonants</u> where you need them.

6) Write out words and explanations <u>in full</u> — use '<u>and</u>' instead of '<u>&</u>' or '<u>+</u>' and <u>don't</u> use '<u>etc</u>' when you could give <u>more examples</u> or a <u>better explanation</u>.

Checking Your Work

Check *for obvious* Punctuation Mistakes

1) Make sure that every sentence <u>starts</u> with a <u>capital letter</u> and <u>ends</u> with a <u>full stop</u>.

2) Don't use <u>exclamation marks</u> unless they're appropriate and you're sure that you need one — chances are, you <u>won't need them</u> at all.

3) Make sure you've added <u>capital letters</u> to words that <u>always</u> need them. Here's a reminder of the most <u>common</u> ones:

> * people
> * towns
> * countries
> * characters
> * religions
> * titles of books, plays etc.

Remember that short words in titles like 'of' and 'and' don't always start with a capital letter.

4) If you've <u>quoted</u> from a text, <u>check</u> the punctuation. There should be <u>speech marks</u> either side of the quote and it should have the <u>same punctuation</u> and <u>capital letters</u> as the <u>original text</u>.

> In Act 2, Scene 2, Juliet says, "Dost thou love me? I know thou wilt say 'ay'" ✗

This doesn't have a lower case letter in the play, so it's wrong.

> In Act 2, Scene 2, Juliet says, "Dost thou love me? I know thou wilt say 'Ay'" ✓

This is better — you need to copy the quote from the original text exactly.

Make sure your Grammar is Correct

1) Check that your writing <u>doesn't</u> sound <u>too chatty</u> — it <u>won't</u> impress the examiner.

> Scout is dead scared of Boo Radley. ✗   Scout is terrified by Boo Radley. ✓

This language is too informal for an essay.   *This language is more appropriate.*

2) There's <u>nothing</u> more confusing than writing which <u>switches</u> between different tenses. You should usually stick to <u>just one tense</u> throughout your answer.

3) Check that you've started a new paragraph every time you talk about a <u>different action</u>, <u>location</u>, <u>person</u>, <u>time</u> or <u>topic</u>. It's <u>important</u> that your essay isn't just one <u>long block of text</u>.

4) Make sure that you haven't used '<u>should of</u>' when you mean '<u>should have</u>' or '<u>don't</u>' when you need '<u>doesn't</u>'.

See p.47-49 for more on paragraphs.

5) If you know that you <u>often</u> get confused between two words, like '<u>it's</u>' and '<u>its</u>', check them <u>extra carefully</u> when you use them in the exam.

Double-check that you've spelt your name right too...

Don't forget to factor in those crucial 5 minutes at the end of the exam to check your work — you'd be surprised how many little mistakes can slip in when you're trying to write your answer under pressure.

How to Correct Mistakes

Picture the scene: you've got 5 minutes 'til the end of the exam, the clock is ticking, and you're checking your work. Suddenly, you spot a mistake. Don't panic — you'll know what to do once you've read this stuff...

Cross Out your mistakes *Neatly*

1) <u>Don't worry</u> if you find a mistake when you <u>check</u> your work. As long as you make your corrections <u>clearly</u>, the examiner <u>won't</u> mark you down.

2) If the mistake is just <u>one word</u> or a <u>short phrase</u>, cross it out <u>neatly</u> and write the correct word <u>above</u> it. Don't just cross out the wrong <u>letters</u> and write that part of the word again, as this <u>won't be clear</u>.

3) Don't write <u>on top of</u> the existing words — it's <u>much better</u> to write the new word above the old one so that the examiner can <u>read</u> your writing.

Don't use correction fluid or eraser pens to correct your work — it'll end up looking messy.

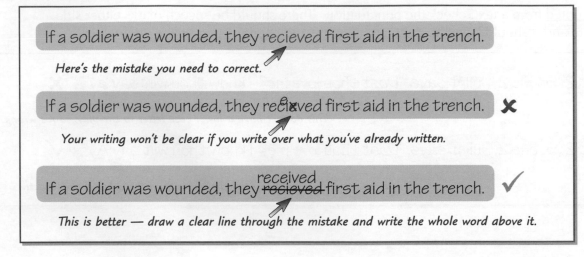

If a soldier was wounded, they recieved first aid in the trench.

Here's the mistake you need to correct.

If a soldier was wounded, they recieved first aid in the trench. ✗

Your writing won't be clear if you write over what you've already written.

If a soldier was wounded, they ~~recieved~~ received first aid in the trench. ✓

This is better — draw a clear line through the mistake and write the whole word above it.

Use a *Double Strike* to show a *New Paragraph*

If you've <u>forgotten</u> to start a <u>new paragraph</u>, use a <u>double strike</u> (like this '//') to show where the new paragraph should <u>begin</u>.

If you've written a plan to help with your essay, every new point needs a new paragraph.

You usually show the start of a paragraph with a new line and an indent

Snowball, Napoleon and Squealer are the "cleverest of the animals". Snowball uses his intelligence to try to improve life on the farm. Because the educated animals were the most powerful on Animal Farm, the fact that Snowball is willing to share power shows how devoted he is to animal equality. // However, the other animals are less educated and they represent the working classes of the Soviet Union. They have no power and believe what they are told without questioning it.

Use a double strike to show that a new paragraph should start here.

How to Correct Mistakes

Use an *Asterisk* to add *Extra Information*

1) If you've <u>missed something out</u>, think about whether you have space to write the missing bit <u>above</u> the line you've already written.

2) If you <u>can</u>, write the missing bit above the line with a '∧' to show <u>exactly where</u> it should go.

"Twinkle, twinkle, little asterisk,
how I wonder what you are(sterisk)…"

> answers
> Eric and Sheila give emotional to the Inspector's questions.

This shows that the word 'answers' is missing after 'emotional'.

Too many asterisks can be confusing — write a plan to make sure you don't forget any important points.

3) If the bit you've missed out <u>won't</u> fit above the line, use an <u>asterisk</u> (like this *) to show the examiner <u>where</u> the missing bit should go.

4) Write the <u>missing words</u> at the <u>end</u> of your essay with another asterisk next to them.

The asterisk shows that something is missing here.

> Sheila is repeatedly told to leave the room by both her parents. The Birlings don't think a young woman should hear this grim story.* Sheila's a young woman who thinks for herself and breaks away from her parents' traditional views.
>
> * However, Sheila stays because she feels it's her duty to find out who's responsible.

Put the asterisk next to the words you want to add.

Cross Out anything you *Don't* want to be *Marked*

1) If you've written something that you <u>don't</u> want the examiner to mark, <u>cross it out neatly</u>.

2) Cross out any <u>notes</u> by the side of your answer. If you don't <u>finish</u> your answer <u>in time</u>, don't cross out your <u>plan</u> — the examiner might look at it to see what you were <u>going to write</u>.

3) If you decide that one of the paragraphs in the <u>middle</u> of your answer is <u>wrong</u>, cross it out clearly so that the examiner <u>knows</u> which <u>bits</u> you don't want them to <u>mark</u>.

4) If you want to <u>cross out one paragraph</u> and <u>replace</u> it with another, use an <u>asterisk</u> and write the new paragraph at the <u>end</u>.

Try not to cross out too much stuff — you might get marks for some of it.

5) Don't <u>scribble things out</u> without thinking — it'll make your essay look <u>messy</u>.

Correct me if I'm wrong, but these pages seem important…

Why yes they are — thank you ever so much for saying so. The main thing to remember is that everyone makes mistakes, but you'll do well in SPaG questions if you can correct your mistakes clearly and neatly.

Rewriting Exercises

Now you know all about checking your work and correcting any mistakes, it's time for you to try your hand at these practice exercises. So flex your SPaG muscles and try these on for size...

You need to **Rewrite** these passages **Correctly**

The answers are at the back of the book.

1) <u>Rewrite</u> each of the passages below and <u>correct</u> the mistakes. There are <u>15 errors</u> in each one.

2) There's one passage for each of the <u>four SPaG subjects</u>: History, English Literature, Geography and RS. Even if you're not studying all four subjects, it's still really <u>good practice</u> to rewrite all the passages.

3) The first three passages test the <u>different</u> SPaG skills <u>separately</u> (spelling, punctuation and grammar), but there are a <u>mixture of errors</u> in the last passage to test that you can check for a <u>combination</u> of mistakes.

4) Aim to correctly identify <u>12 or more errors</u> per passage. If you spot <u>fewer than 12 errors</u> on one of the first three passages, use your scores to <u>identify</u> which <u>areas of SPaG</u> you need to <u>look at again</u>.

This passage only contains **Spelling Errors**

During World War I, many women had the oportunity to work for the first time. Men's jobs were suddenley available cos they were away fighting and women were happy to take them, partly to prove that they where just as capable as men. Women worked as bus conductors and farm workers, and took tecnical jobs in engineering workshops. The women who worked in factorys that made esential goods for the war, like weapons an uniforms, had a direct affect on the war effort. Women also joined women's branchs of the armed forces and nursed wounded soldiers in millitary hospitals.

As a result, people's attitudes towards women and their rights began too change. Before the war, women could not vote, but many people beleived that women shoud have equal rights to men. A group called the suffragettes started to campain for a new law.

Correct the **Punctuation** and **Capital Letter Errors** in this passage

Calpurnia is an important character in 'To Kill a mockingbird' because she is the link between the white and black communitie's. Calpurnia takes Jem and Scout to her church, which teaches the children about the black community! The congregation is generally friendly towards Scout and Jem until one of it's members (Lula confronts Calpurnia and tells her, You ain't got no business bringin' white chillun here". This shows that calpurnia's closeness to a white, family can cause problems for her However, most people think that she is a supportive friend to both: communities. For example, she supports Atticus by going with him to tell Helen robinson about her husbands death.

Calpurnia also helps to bring up Atticus's children. She can be strict, but she treats Scout kindly, calling her names like "baby" and "honey. the fact that Atticus trusts Calpurnia with his childrens' upbringing shows that she is part of their family.

Rewriting Exercises

Look for **Grammar Errors** in this passage

Remember that grammar includes things like verb tenses and agreement, as well as pronouns and paragraphs.

Climate change is any change in the weather of an area over a long period. Scientists which study climate change know that the Earth are getting warmer because they has been using thermometers to measure the Earth's temperature over the last 150 years. Their measurements indicate that the Earth is getting warmer more rapidly than it does in the past. An increase in global temperature is called global warming. It is one of a number of types of widespread climate change.

There are other evidence which shows that the Earth is getting warmer. The Antarctic ice sheets are melting, what causes sea levels to risen. This means that oceans expands and it leads to flooding in coastal areas. Most scientists thinks that global warming must of been largely caused by human activity. The main cause of global warming is an increase in greenhouse gases. Greenhouse gases in the Earth's atmosphere trap heat that is reflect off the Earth's surface. This mean that less of the heat escape and the Earth was warming up.

There are a **Mixture** of **SPaG Errors** in this passage

Religion is an inportant part of all societies around the world. Even though it might only seem relevant to the people what practise the religion, it provide certain values, and society would not of developed in the same way without it.

Some societies are secular: religion and government are kept completely separate. In a secular society, people are free to follow a religious faith if we want to, but they don't have to follow any religion The government won't take religious beliefs into account when it makes decisions passes laws or spends taxs. Some people believe that this is a fair system because it doesn't give preference to followers of won faith.

Even if a society is secular, religious festivals still play an important role. For example, many people choose to celebrate christmas or Hanukkah. These celebrations can brought people together and give believers and non-believers a sense of comunity. Non-religious people can enjoy events that have been organising by a religious group or take part in it's activitys.

If you want to give yourself some realistic exam practice, give yourself 5 minutes to find the mistakes.

Re-e-write — when the crowd say 'bo', correct it...

Hooray, well done and celebrations all round — you've reached the end of the book. If you found one of these passages particularly tricky, look back over the sections and remind yourself of anything you missed.

ANSWERS

Answers

Page 3 (Practice Questions)
1) classes
2) cities
3) children
4) teeth
5) churches
6) claws
7) volcanoes
8) lives
9) discos
10) beliefs
11) deer
12) ladies

Page 5 (Practice Questions)
1) innumerable
2) disapprove
3) unnecessary
4) procreation
5) untimely
6) immaturity
7) submarine
8) irrelevant

1) successful
2) forgetting
3) thoughtless
4) conquered
5) budgeted
6) forgotten
7) beginner
8) followed

Page 7 (Practice Questions)
1) government
2) debt
3) believe
4) ascended
5) species
6) could
7) when
8) atheists
9) subtle
10) deity
11) separately
12) scientific

Page 9 (Practice Questions)
1) 'Romeo and Juliet' is more popular than 'Macbeth' in schools, maybe because the story is better.
2) In Geography, the best way to get a better mark than my friends is to do the most studying.
3) China has the largest population in the world, with more than 1.3 billion people.
4) Morale was very important in the trenches — happier soldiers meant more effective offensives.

Page 11 (Practice Questions)
1) I may be able to help, but then again maybe not.
2) Is there any way to drill into the depths of the deepest glaciers?
3) I was altogether confused by her attempt to turn a rabbit into a dove.
4) They came in to investigate everybody's alibis.

Page 13 (Practice Questions)
1) Their aim was to avoid the impact of war, but it still had an effect on the country.
2) In the past, Jews were discouraged from marrying someone from another religious faith.
3) The Inspector is a plot device designed to force the Birlings to accept their wrongdoings.
4) It is important to practise emergency drills in countries where earthquakes are common.

Page 15 (Practice Questions)
1) It was thought that $30 billion was lost within two days as a result of the Wall Street Crash.
2) The values in 'To Kill a Mockingbird' will teach you a lot because many of them are still relevant.
3) Our research into renewable energy has been very thorough in the last few years.

4) The teachings of Judaism and Islam are against euthanasia. Catholics are opposed to it too.

Page 17 (Practice Questions)
Answers may vary, e.g. strengths = Sometimes The Right Elephant Never Gets The Ham Sandwich.

Page 19 (Practice Questions)
1) misspelt
2) shelves
3) supposed
4) progressing
5) ceiling
6) alphabetical
7) accept
8) seize
9) insightful
10) brushes
11) criticism
12) although

Page 21 (Practice Questions)
1) In 1941, President Roosevelt gave an important speech.
2) It can be very cold in Norway during December.
3) Which characters sometimes speak in Latin?
4) The boys asked whether they could play outside the school.

Page 23 (Practice Questions)
1) The prophets, Moses and Elijah, appeared out of nowhere.
2) Germany, France, Spain and Italy are European countries.
3) Unlike most authors at the time, Jane Austen wrote about women.
4) The French Prime Minister, the British Prime Minister and the President were in agreement.
5) The children, who had studied the novel, failed to understand it.
6) The USA and USSR, despite their history, became allies.

Page 25 (Practice Questions)
1) Elizabeth I was the daughter of Henry VIII and Anne Boleyn (his second wife).
2) Boxer (a cart-horse) is a determined and loyal worker on the farm.
3) CAFOD (Catholic Agency for Overseas Development) is a religious charity.
4) There is a consensus (general agreement) that glacial retreat is caused by global warming.

Page 27 (Practice Questions)
1) Repainting the church's walls will cost thousands of pounds.
2) "There's nothing to worry about," said the teacher.
3) The wolves' habitat is being destroyed by urban growth.
4) The people in the town were impressed by the policemen's actions.

Page 29 (Practice Questions)
1) The soil had nutrients, but its top layer was thin.
2) Sometimes it's difficult to understand poetry.
3) Look for the symbols on its walls.
4) I think it's been snowing heavily.

Page 31 (Practice Questions)

Answers may vary, e.g. a short quote from a novel = In Chapter 1 Lennie is described as being <u>"like a terrier"</u> when he is holding the mouse.

Page 33 (Practice Questions)

1) Cyclone Nargis was devastating; <u>its</u> path of destruction left people short of food.
2) Stalin made the US go to war, which made <u>them</u> realise <u>he</u> was a threat.
3) Catholics believe the Pope is infallible; <u>they</u> believe <u>he</u> represents God.
4) Lady Macbeth planned to kill Duncan, but <u>she</u> didn't kill <u>him</u> herself.

Page 35 (Practice Questions)

1) Wordsworth is one of the authors <u>whom</u> we can thank for the birth of Romanticism.
2) There is still debate over <u>who's</u> responsible for the assassination of President Kennedy.
3) One campaigner <u>who</u> is very famous Is Martin Luther King, <u>whose</u> words inspired thousands.
4) The Pope, <u>who's</u> the leader of the Catholic church, said <u>that</u> contraception is immoral.

Page 37 (Practice Questions)

1) She <u>goes</u> to every play that she can. It <u>is</u> a time-consuming hobby, but I <u>think</u> it's worth it.
2) You <u>try</u> very hard to get good marks. I <u>hope</u> that I <u>revise</u> enough to do just as well.
3) My brother and I <u>are</u> interested in physics. He often <u>flies</u> his kite to study the effect of gravity.
4) My teacher <u>tells</u> us that the novel <u>takes</u> some understanding, but its message <u>is</u> important.

Page 39 (Practice Questions)

1) buying	5) shaking	9) getting
2) clapping	6) lying	10) braking
3) waiting	7) digging	11) winning
4) dancing	8) driving	12) beginning

Page 41 (Practice Questions)

1) He <u>has begun</u>	4) We <u>have had</u>	7) It <u>has eaten</u>
2) It <u>has hidden</u>	5) We <u>have visited</u>	8) It <u>has broken</u>
3) They <u>have done</u>	6) She <u>has stolen</u>	

Page 43 (Practice Questions)

1) They shouldn't <u>have</u> done that, because it got me into trouble. I might <u>have</u> been given detention.
2) You could <u>have</u> helped us finish dessert. We couldn't finish it because of the amount of sugar in it.
3) The flooding may <u>have</u> been caused by lots of heavy rain falling on the hills and mountains.

Page 45 (Practice Questions)

1) She <u>doesn't</u> like me, and her brother <u>doesn't</u> like me either.
2) I <u>don't</u> enjoy eating cabbage, but Kitty <u>doesn't</u> enjoy eating peas.
3) Ella and Kamal <u>don't</u> have a pet, and I <u>don't</u> have a bike.
4) Frank <u>doesn't</u> want to go to the cinema, but you <u>don't</u> like going on your own.

Page 47 (Practice Questions)

1) When the birth rate is higher than the death rate, the population of a country <u>grows</u>.
2) A 'Holy War' <u>is</u> a war where people believe that God is 'on their side'.
3) George <u>decides</u> to look after Lennie because he feels sorry for him.
4) Religion can help to bring families together, but it can also <u>cause</u> conflict.

Page 49 (Practice Questions)

Hitler was able to control the lives of German people between 1933 and 1939 by using a range of methods. After 1933 all political parties other than the Nazis were banned. Communist and socialist leaders who stayed in Germany were arrested, and those who could went into exile elsewhere in Europe.
(This paragraph is about the <u>repression of political parties</u>.)

The Nazis set up a series of concentration camps for all their political opponents and these were soon used to imprison other groups in society who did not fit in with Hitler's vision of a pure German race. A system soon developed where people could be arrested and questioned without any real cause.
(This paragraph is about <u>concentration camps</u>.)

Propaganda was also a key factor. The Party controlled all public information and nothing could be broadcast on radio, shown in cinemas or printed in newspapers unless it had been approved. The school system, youth groups and all other cultural activities were all linked to the Nazi propaganda machine.
(This paragraph is about <u>propaganda</u>.)

Page 54 (Spelling Passage)

During World War I, many women had the <u>oportunity</u> to work for the first time. Men's jobs were <u>suddenley</u> available <u>cos</u> they were away fighting and women were happy to take them, partly to prove that they <u>where</u> just as capable as men. Women worked as bus conductors and farm workers, and took <u>tecnical</u> jobs in engineering workshops. The women who worked in <u>factorys</u> that made <u>esential</u> goods for the war, like weapons <u>an</u> uniforms, had a direct <u>affect</u> on the war effort. Women also joined women's <u>branchs</u> of the armed forces and nursed wounded soldiers in <u>millitary</u> hospitals.
As a result, people's attitudes towards women and their rights began <u>too</u> change. Before the war, women could not vote, but many people <u>beleived</u> that women <u>shoud</u> have equal rights to men. A group called the suffragettes started to <u>campain</u> for a new law.

1) **opportunity** — 'opportunity' is spelt with a double 'p'.
2) **suddenly** — the suffix added to 'sudden' is 'ly' — there is no 'e' after the 'l'.
3) **because** — 'cos' is text speak; 'because' is more appropriate.
4) **were** — 'were' is correct because it is the past tense of the verb 'to be'; 'where' is a word relating to location and doesn't make sense in this context.
5) **technical** — there is a silent 'h' in the word 'technical'.
6) **factories** — words ending in a consonant and 'y', drop the 'y' and take the plural ending '-ies'.
7) **essential** — 'essential' is spelt with a double 's'.
8) **and** — 'and' is correct because it is a connective.
9) **effect** — 'affect' is a verb; in this context you need to use the noun 'effect'.
10) **branches** — words ending in 'ch' take the plural ending '-es'.
11) **military** — 'military' is spelt with only one 'l'.

12) **to** — 'to' is correct because it is part of the verb phrase 'to change'; 'too' means 'in excess' or 'also'.

13) **believed** — this word follows the rule 'i before e'.

14) **should** — 'should' is spelt with a silent 'l'.

15) **campaign** — 'campaign' is spelt with a silent 'g'.

Page 54 (Punctuation Passage)

Calpurnia is an important character in 'To Kill a <u>mockingbird</u>' because she is the link between the white and black <u>communitie's</u>. Calpurnia takes Jem and Scout to her church, which teaches the children about the black community<u>!</u> The congregation is generally friendly towards Scout and Jem until one of <u>it's</u> members (<u>Lula</u> confronts Calpurnia and tells her,<u>_You</u> ain't got no business bringin' white chillun here". This shows that <u>calpurnia's</u> closeness to a <u>white, family</u> can cause problems for <u>her</u> However, most people think that she is a supportive friend to <u>both: communities</u>. For example, she supports Atticus by going with him to tell Helen <u>robinson</u> about her <u>husbands</u> death.

Calpurnia also helps to bring up Atticus's children. She can be strict, but she treats Scout kindly, calling her names like "baby" and <u>"honey</u>. <u>the</u> fact that Atticus trusts Calpurnia with his <u>childrens'</u> upbringing shows that she is part of their family.

1) **Mockingbird** — titles of books are spelt with capital letters, apart from tiny words like 'a'.

2) **communities** — 'communities' doesn't need an apostrophe because there are no missing letters and the word is not showing possession.

3) **community.** — this sentence should end with a full stop.

4) **its** — the member belongs to the congregation, so you should use 'its' — 'it's' means 'it is' or 'it has'.

5) **(Lula)** — a closing bracket is needed after 'Lula'.

6) **"You** — there needs to be a quotation mark at the start of a quote.

7) **Calpurnia's** — people's names are spelt with a capital letter.

8) **white family** — there doesn't need to be a comma between 'white' and 'family' because it is not a list, two separate points in a sentence or two adjectives changing a noun in a similar way.

9) **her.** — a full stop is needed at the end of a sentence.

10) **both communities** — a colon isn't needed between 'both' and 'communities' because it's not introducing more information.

11) **Robinson** — surnames are spelt with a capital letter.

12) **husband's** — there needs to be an apostrophe before the 's'.

13) **honey"** — a quotation mark is needed at the end of a quote.

14) **The** — a capital letter is needed at the start of a sentence.

15) **children's** — 'children' is already plural, so the apostrophe needs to go before the 's'.

Page 55 (Grammar Passage)

Climate change is any change in the weather of an area over a long period. Scientists <u>which</u> study climate change know that the Earth <u>are</u> getting warmer because they <u>has</u> been using thermometers to measure the Earth's temperature over the last 150 years. Their measurements indicate that the Earth is getting warmer more rapidly than it <u>does</u> in the past. An increase in global temperature is called global warming. It is one of a number of types of widespread climate change.

There <u>are</u> other evidence which shows that the Earth is getting warmer. The Antarctic ice sheets are melting, <u>what</u> causes sea levels to <u>risen</u>. This means that oceans <u>expands</u> and it leads to flooding in coastal areas. <u>Most</u> scientists <u>thinks</u> that global warming must <u>of</u> been largely caused by human activity. The main cause of global warming is an increase in greenhouse gases. Greenhouse gases in the Earth's atmosphere trap heat that is <u>reflect</u> off the Earth's surface. This <u>mean</u> that less of the heat <u>escape</u> and the Earth <u>was</u> warming up.

1) **who** — this should be 'who' (or 'that') because it refers to people.

2) **is** — this should be 'is' as 'the Earth' is singular.

3) **have** — this should be 'have' because it is in the past tense and it should agree with the third person pronoun 'they'.

4) **did** — this should be 'did' or 'has' as this is in the past tense.

5) **is** — this should be 'is' as it is in the present tense and 'evidence' is singular.

6) **which** — this should be 'which' because it is connecting two sentences.

7) **rise** — this should be 'rise' as it is an infinitive.

8) **expand** — this should be 'expand' as it is in the present tense and agrees with the subject 'oceans', which is plural.

9) **Most** — there needs to be a new paragraph between 'coastal areas.' and 'Most' because a new point is being made.

10) **think** — this should be 'think' as it is in the present tense and agrees with the subject 'scientists', which is plural.

11) **have** — use 'have' because it follows the verb 'must' (or replace 'must of been' with 'is being').

12) **reflected** — this should be 'reflected' because it is in the past.

13) **means** — this should be 'means' because it is a third person singular present verb.

14) **escapes** — this should be 'escapes' because 'heat' is singular.

15) **is** — this should be 'is' because it is in the present tense.

Page 55 (SPaG Passage)

Religion is an <u>inportant</u> part of all societies around the world. Even though it might only seem relevant to the people <u>what</u> practise the religion, it <u>provide</u> certain values, and society would not <u>of</u> developed in the same way without it.

Some societies are secular: religion and government are kept completely separate. In a secular society, people are free to follow a religious faith if <u>we</u> want to, but they don't have to follow any <u>religion</u> The government won't take religious beliefs into account when it makes <u>decisions</u> passes laws or spends <u>taxs</u>. Some people believe that this is a fair system because it doesn't give preference to followers of <u>won</u> faith.

Even if a society is secular, religious festivals still play an important role. For example, many people choose to celebrate <u>christmas</u> or Hanukkah. These celebrations can <u>brought</u> people together and give believers and non-believers a sense of <u>comunity</u>. Non-religious people can enjoy events that have been <u>organising</u> by a religious group or take part in <u>it's</u> <u>activitys</u>.

1) **important** — this word is spelt with an 'm'.

2) **who** — this should be 'who' (or 'that') because it is referring to people.

3) **provides** — this should be 'provides' because it is a third person singular present verb.

4) **have** — use 'have' because it follows the verb 'wouldn't'.

5) **they** — the text is written in the third person, so the pronoun should be 'they'.

6) **religion.** — a full stop is needed to end a sentence.

7) **decisions,** — 'decisions' is part of a list, so there should be a comma to separate it from the other items.

8) **taxes** — words ending in 'x' take '-es' to make them plural.

9) **one** — this should be 'one' as this is a number.

10) **Christmas** — the names of festivals are spelt with a capital letter.

11) **bring** — this should be 'bring' as it is an infinitive.

12) **community** — 'community' is spelt with a double 'm'.

13) **organised** — this should be 'organised' as it's in the past.

14) **its** — the activities 'belong' to the religious groups, so you should use 'its'.

15) **activities** — words ending in a consonant and 'y', drop the 'y' and take the plural ending '-ies'.

Glossary

adjective	A word that <u>describes</u> a <u>noun</u>, e.g. "<u>beautiful</u> morning", "<u>frosty</u> lawn".
adverb	A word that <u>describes</u> a <u>verb</u>, e.g. "run <u>quickly</u>", "dance <u>happily</u>".
apostrophe	A mark (') which shows that letters are <u>missing</u>, e.g. "We have" = "<u>We've</u>". Apostrophes can also show <u>possession</u> of something, e.g. "Fred's apple".
comparative	A word that <u>compares</u> one thing with another, e.g. "<u>shorter</u>", "<u>worse</u>".
connective	A word that <u>joins</u> two clauses or sentences, e.g. "<u>and</u>", "<u>but</u>", "<u>therefore</u>".
homophones	Words that <u>sound the same</u>, but mean different things, e.g. "<u>hair</u>" and "<u>hare</u>".
infinitive verb	The most <u>basic form</u> of a verb with the word '<u>to</u>' in <u>front</u> of it e.g. "<u>to see</u>".
irregular plural	Plurals which are <u>not</u> formed using <u>standard patterns</u>, e.g. "man" becomes "<u>men</u>".
irregular verb	Verbs which are <u>not</u> formed using <u>standard patterns</u>, e.g. "to do" becomes "<u>did</u>" in the past, and "to fight" becomes "<u>fought</u>" in the past.
long vowel sound	A vowel sound which is longer than a short vowel, e.g. the vowel sound in "sl<u>o</u>pe" is long, whereas the vowel sound in "sl<u>o</u>p" is short.
main verb	The <u>most important</u> verb in a sentence, e.g. "He will be playing" — "<u>playing</u>" is the main verb because it has the <u>strongest meaning</u> in the sentence.
negative	Words like "<u>no</u>", "<u>not</u>" and "<u>nothing</u>" that <u>reverse</u> the meaning of a statement, e.g. "He is playing" becomes "He is <u>not</u> playing".
noun	A word that <u>names</u> something, e.g. "<u>Paul</u>", "<u>scissors</u>", "<u>flock</u>", "<u>loyalty</u>".
plural	A type of <u>noun</u> that tells you there is <u>more than one</u> of something, e.g. "<u>rocks</u>".
prefix	Letters that can be put <u>in front</u> of a word to <u>change its meaning</u>, e.g. "<u>un</u>lock".
preposition	A word that tells you how things are <u>related</u>, e.g. "<u>in</u>", "<u>above</u>", "<u>before</u>".
pronoun	Words that can be used <u>instead</u> of <u>nouns</u>, e.g. "<u>I</u>", "<u>you</u>", "<u>he</u>", "<u>it</u>".
regular plural	Plurals which follow a <u>standard pattern</u>, e.g. add '<u>s</u>' to "cat" to make the plural, "<u>cats</u>".
regular verb	Verbs which are formed using a <u>standard pattern</u>, e.g. adding the simple past tense ending "<u>-ed</u>" — "play" becomes "<u>played</u>" in the past.
short vowel sound	A vowel sound which is shorter than a long vowel, e.g. the vowel sound in "k<u>e</u>pt" is short, whereas the vowel sound in "k<u>ee</u>p" is long.
stressed syllable	The <u>part</u> of the word that you <u>say</u> with <u>more emphasis</u> e.g. "<u>vi</u>sit".
subject	The part of the sentence that the verb <u>agrees with</u>. It's usually the <u>person</u> or <u>thing doing</u> the action of a verb, e.g. "<u>Jo</u> laughed", "<u>the bird</u> flew".
suffix	Letters that can be put <u>after</u> a word to <u>change its meaning</u>, e.g. "play<u>ful</u>".
superlative	A word that refers to the <u>most</u> or <u>least</u> of a group of things, e.g. "the <u>best</u> team".
syllable	A word, or part of a word, which can be said in a <u>single sound</u>, e.g. "beautiful" has <u>three</u> syllables, "<u>beau-ti-ful</u>".
tense	A verb's tense tells you whether something is in the <u>past</u>, <u>present</u> or <u>future</u>, e.g. "I <u>have had</u> a bath" = past tense, "I am <u>having</u> a bath" = present tense, "I <u>will have</u> a bath" = future tense.
verb	An <u>action</u> or <u>being</u> word, e.g. "I <u>run</u>", "he <u>went</u>", "you <u>are</u>".

Index